Bridging the Business-Project Divide

For Emilia

Bridging the Business-Project Divide

Techniques for Reconciling Business-as-Usual and Project Cultures

JOHN BRINKWORTH

Routledge
Taylor & Francis Group

LONDON AND NEW YORK

First published in paperback 2024

First published 2014 by Gower Publishing

Published 2016 by Routledge
4 Park Square, Milton Park, Abingdon, Oxon OX14 4RN

and by Routledge
605 Third Avenue, New York, NY 10158

Routledge is an imprint of the Taylor & Francis Group, an informa business

British Library Cataloguing in Publication Data
A catalogue record for this book is available from the British Library

Library of Congress Cataloging-in-Publication Data
Brinkworth, John W. O.
  Bridging the business-project divide : techniques for reconciling business-as-usual and project cultures / by John Brinkworth.
     pages cm
  Includes bibliographical references and index.
  ISBN 978-1-4094-6517-1 (hbk) -- ISBN 978-1-4094-6518-8 (ebook) -- ISBN 978-1-4094-6519-5 (epub) 1. Project management. I. Title.
  HD69.P75B755 2014
  658.4'04--dc23
                                                                                    2014006121

ISBN: 978-1-4094-6517-1 (hbk)
ISBN: 978-1-03-283749-9 (pbk)
ISBN: 978-1-315-56993-2 (ebk)

DOI: 10.4324/9781315569932

Contents

List of Figures and Tables

Figures

Tables

About the Author

John Brinkworth is a management consultant who assists organisations to improve their processes for project and programme management. He is also part of the associate faculty at Henley Business School. He is a Member of the Institute of Directors (IoD), a Fellow of the Chartered Management Institute, a Certified Management Consultant (CMC®), a Chartered IT Professional and an Associate of the Chartered Quality Institute. He has previously published a book on Software Quality Management, via Prentice Hall, in the early 1990s. He has more recently had articles published in *Conspectus* and *Project Manager Today*, and for the then UK Office of Government Commerce (OGC) served on their review team for a range of their publications relating to programme and project management.

Preface

What This Book Is

This book is deliberately practical and pragmatic. It is based on the professional experience of the author covering nearly 30 years of project-related work and consulting. It is partisan in the sense that it is the distillation of the author's observations, experiences and insights. Its aim is to be of direct use to both business and project professionals. It is written so as to be applicable to all types of project and thus uses neutral language which is slightly abstract – in particular adopting terms such as 'problem' and 'solution'.

Its fundamental aim is to provide each community with an insight into the thinking and approaches used by the other. The aspiration is that by unpacking and explaining these paradigms, members of the 'other camp' will gain an insight into 'how the other half thinks'. As a result, they will be in a position to build an atmosphere and approach of increased positive understanding and cooperation towards the achievement of a shared goal.

What This Book Is Not

This book is not an academic treatise, not a consolidation of the state of the field of knowledge, not a formal text book. It is not the integration of many academic studies and other sources of work. It does not include multiple footnotes and extensive references to a large number of other books and publications. There are plenty of fine books that already do that – but this is not one of them.

It does not 'take sides' between the business viewpoint and the project viewpoint. Although it is written by someone who has spent their working life in the 'project world', particularly information technology (IT), so it may include accidental biases, it is hoped that these have been removed. Those that inadvertently remain are not intentional.

It is not meant to be read from cover to cover. Most readers will be at a particular stage in a project or come from a particular specialism. The relevant chapters covering that lifecycle phase and that specialism may be all that they read. That is OK – the book will still have served its purpose. With this in mind, certain central ideas are presented more than once. Reading the book from start to finish will lead to these points becoming clear. The book may even start to feel a bit repetitious. That is perfectly understandable, but considering the fact that repetition remains one of the best ways of learning, the repeated presentation of some key concepts should help them to become more apparent to the reader who does work their way through from beginning to end. Each chapter finishes with a summary of its key points, providing an aide-memoire on what has been discussed.

John Brinkworth
June 2014

Disclaimer

This book is presented solely for educational purposes. The author and publisher are not offering it as legal, accounting, project management, business or other professional services advice. While best efforts have been used in preparing this book, the author and publisher make no representations or warranties of any kind and assume no liabilities of any kind with respect to the accuracy or completeness of the contents and specifically disclaim any implied warranties of merchantability or fitness of use for a particular purpose. Neither the author nor the publisher shall be held liable or responsible to any person or entity with respect to any loss or incidental or consequential damages caused, or alleged to have been caused, directly or indirectly, by the information or material contained herein. No warranty may be created or extended by sales representatives or written sales materials. Every organisation is different and the advice and strategies contained herein may not be suitable for your situation. You should seek the services of a competent professional before beginning any project, change or improvement programme.

Acknowledgements

This book would not have been possible without the time, energy and support of a number of people to whom I wish to record my thanks. Jonathan Norman, my commissioning editor at Gower, for his positive response to my initial idea for the book, and his dedicated and thoughtful assistance during the writing and production process. Thanks also go to the rest of the team at Gower, notably Melisa Young, Fiona Martin, Christine Muddiman, Adam Guppy, Jon Lloyd, Sara Hutton, Susan White, Michelle Spencer, Liz Matravers, Tracey Daborn, and Donna Shanks.

My reviewers, Mike Brooks, Peter Race and Paul Lawrence, all provided helpful comments and suggestions for adjustments to the book, a number of which I have taken on board. The quality of the book has been improved as a result, and I am grateful for their time and considered input. This is a book based on personal experience, so I have been selective in responding to review comments. Any shortcomings that remain in the book are mine and no reflection upon the quality of my reviewers' advice.

Finally, I must thank my wife for her patience, encouragement and support. Writing a book can take a considerable slice of time and focus away from the other areas of one's life, and her support has been invaluable.

List of Abbreviations

I have deliberately attempted to write a book that is accessible, and so have minimised the abbreviations and acronyms within it. The ones I do use are as follows:

CEO   Chief Executive Officer
HR   Human Resources
IT   Information Technology
NPV   Net Present Value
PID   Project Initiation Document
PO   Project Office
RoI   Return on Investment
T&M   Time and Materials

Chapter 1

Introduction

The Divide

Business and projects tend not to mix. They do not even understand each other. This often leads to problems. But what causes to this to happen?

There are two mindsets in operation these days in most organisations. They relate to the two worlds of:

- 'business as usual', which this book will refer to as 'business'; and

- project management, which involves the delivery of a change using a project approach.

The Business Viewpoint

'Business' for the purposes of this book covers any sort of organisation or enterprise. It can be private sector, public sector or charity. What is significant here is that the organisation is focused on delivering something on an ongoing basis. It might make a product, maybe a range of products – which could be tangible or electronic; alternatively, it might provide a service. What matters is that it plans to continue to provide the product or service for the foreseeable future.

Over time, the product might change – a car manufacturer will bring out new models, a bank may offer a new type of bank account – but their business of making cars or looking after people's money will continue indefinitely.

This expectation of a continued existence, with business stretching out over the horizon, leads to a particular way of seeing and running the organisation. Organisational structures are established and people have roles that create, support and manage the products or services. A career path develops, with the opportunity to gain skills and expertise in a particular area and over time be promoted within the organisation to take on more responsibilities. These structures, even if the post-holders change, develop a degree of permanence. There is an expectation that there will always be a CEO, a Finance Director, and a Head of Sales.

A timetable for the business evolves. The calendar tends to drive this with annual budgets, quarterly sales targets and weekly management meetings. The calendar sets up a heartbeat for the management control of the organisation. Overlaying this is a second tempo that relates to the product or service. It is driven by how long it takes to create a unit of product or service. A restaurant that serves lunches starts with raw ingredients at 9 am and finishes with empty plates by 2 pm. A car manufacturer may take two to three days to make an individual car, but due to the production line nature of the assembly work, many cars will be made each day. A call centre can handle hundreds of enquiries, each lasting just two or three minutes, every day.

These organisation structures and timetables set the framework for how the business runs. They give a set of reference points and familiarity to what happens each day, each month and across a year. There may be variation in the nature of the work, for example, finance departments preparing budgets at one point during the year and putting together annual reports for shareholders at a different time. Manufacturing runs may vary, with a clothing company producing different ranges of garments for the summer season and for the winter season. Airlines may have busy Mondays and Fridays when they fly a lot of business passengers and a different mix of travellers during weekends and school holidays. In all cases, however, the basic pattern of providing a product or service on an ongoing basis sits at the heart of the business viewpoint of an organisation.

The Project Viewpoint

Projects are different. They have a start and a finish. The people undertaking the project may not have worked together before the start of the project. The project will have a particular objective. It exists to change something.

That change can have a range of manifestations. It might be a building or a road or a railway that is constructed. It could be a new computer system that is being delivered. There might be a change to an organisation – a merger or a separation. There could be a new department that is created. The project is undertaken by a team, brought together for the purpose, and its outputs and changes are delivered to a client and in some cases a set of users.

For convenience in this book, we will describe a project as delivering a solution. This does have connotations related to the world of information technology (IT), but here we will use it in its most general sense – the addressing of a set of requirements by providing a solution to a need for a change.

The key point about a project is that the project is not part of the business-as-usual operation for the organisation.

The project team are subject to different pressures from the business team. The members of the team need to be assembled, they need to have clarity on what is required to be achieved, and they need to get hold of the means to effect the desired changes and make their deliverables. The project has a cost – each day it exists, it absorbs money that the organisation would otherwise have used elsewhere. This puts a time pressure on to the project. Some projects have 'immovable deadlines' – classic examples include creating a new sports facility in time for a particular tournament or fixing a problem such as the 'millennium bug', which needed to be resolved before 1 January 2000. Other projects have deadlines which could slip, but would involve additional costs and considerable loss of face for their sponsors.

Projects tend to be staffed by people who live in a 'project universe'. They work on a series of projects, moving from one to the next. Sometimes they work for a provider of project services (e.g. a consultancy, a software house, or a road building company), while at other times they may be freelance and hired separately for each project. They are familiar with the project rhythm of start-up, design, build, test and deploy, which can take a few weeks or may spread over a number of years.

This lifecycle does not align to the periodic heartbeat of the business-as-usual organisation.

The Interaction between the Two Worlds

This split has a number of effects. The business part of the organisation often houses the recipients of the project. This can happen in a number of different ways. They may be the users of a new computer system or they may be the subject of a restructuring, with some staff being made redundant. In addition, some of them can become involved in the project. The degree of involvement will vary, they might be consulted about the requirements for the change, they might be part of the team testing the new system or they might be recruited as 'change champions' to help get their colleagues to work in a different way.

These interactions sit at the overlapping boundary of the two worlds. Both viewpoints can have difficulty appreciating where the other team is coming from. What is obvious and normal to a member of the business team (e.g. you cannot make a change during the busiest month of the trading year) would not necessarily occur to a project person. What is clear to a project person (e.g. that changing the requirements after agreeing them will delay the project by a number of months) may seem unreasonable to a member of the business team.

These differences of perspective can then be magnified by the time pressure that faces all projects. Delays, challenges and differences of opinion, whilst resolvable in the cold light of day, can be blown out of proportion during the heated process of keeping a complex project on track whilst not disrupting the business into which it is going to deliver.

The Aim of this Book

So what can be done? That is what this book seeks to address. How can the friction at the interface between the business world and the project world be reduced?

Projects follow a fairly standard lifecycle and have a number of considerations that they keep in mind for their duration (such as quality, finances and risk). This book considers each project stage and each project strand from both a business-as-usual perspective and from a project perspective. It then looks at how the differing perspectives can be brought closer together.

Readers from each world should recognise themselves and their viewpoint, and in addition gain a few 'ah-ha' moments as they get an insight into how the other half thinks.

It is hoped that this will bridge the divide, enabling project teams and business teams to understand each other better and, as a result, to achieve more successful projects together.

PART I
The Project Lifecycle

Chapter 2
Identifying a Project

The Business Perspective

When do businesses want to undertake a project? It may seem that projects are happening all around, but what is the underlying reason for a project to be performed?

Something needs to be changed.

Nothing stays the same for long in the world; external events, problems, challenges and uncertainties can all lead to the need to undertake a project. It is worth noting that more often than not, it is the business part of an organisation that initiates a project.

Organisational changes can often prompt many types of project – mergers, separations, new business units or a restructuring of an existing business.

Activity changes can also lead to a project. This can be a new activity. It could also be an existing activity where some characteristic of it needs to be changed, a new method for doing it, the volume of the activity – scaling up to more production, cutting back for less. The activity itself might remain the same in terms of what is provided to the end-client, but the systems that support it might need to be changed.

Sometimes a suite of projects may be undertaken as part of implementing an organisation's strategy. The identification will have already been done as part of putting together the strategy. This may include creating a schedule of projects grouped into a portfolio.

There are other situations when sometimes it is an existing project team, or maybe an external supplier, that approaches an organisation and persuades it to undertake a project. But even in this case, the project identification will be undertaken by the business. In short, unless the business agrees that the project is needed, it will not happen.

The Project Perspective

The project perspective on identifying a project is associated more with a number of factors that the early members of the project team need to know as soon as possible.

Who will be the sponsor?

From the point of view of the project team, who is their client? This may well be different from the recipients and users of what the project delivers.

What is the scope of the project? What will it do and what will it change? Where is the boundary line, what will it not change or deliver? Are there any other related projects that will also be making changes at the same time? Does the project rely on any of these other projects for inputs?

What are the actual deliverables? This is the core essence of the project from the project team's perspective.

What are the timescales – when does the project need to be finished? Are all the deliverables provided at the same time?

What methods will the project follow? These can include widely available good practice management methods (such as PRINCE2® (TSO for AXELOS 2009),[1] Managing Successful Programmes – MSP® (TSO for AXELOS 2011)),[2] but also organisation-specific ways of working. Does the business impose these methods explicitly on the project? Is there an implicit assumption from the business that the project will work in a particular way?

Determining whether an organisation is effectively operating in a way that matches its strategic goals is an important early step for a project. Strategic goals can relate to how the current day-to-day business functions, what it does and provides. Separately they can also cover how the business wants to grow

---

1   PRINCE2® is a registered trade mark of AXELOS Limited.
2   MSP® is a registered trade mark of AXELOS Limited.

or change, what it wants to be or do differently and when it wants this change to happen. The members of the project team need to gain clarity on this as soon as possible so that they are able to shape the project accordingly.

Bridging the Divide

Identifying a project may appear obvious to many. However, to avoid a gap opening up between the business and project teams right from the start, a number of aspects are worth addressing.

Clarify the scope as much as possible – what is within scope and expected to be delivered, what is on the edge and may or may not form part of the final deliverables, and what is definitely out-of-scope and not being provided by the project? This final out-of-scope category can be the trickiest, as different stakeholders, across the business and also at the business-project boundary, will tend to have different tacit assumptions about what is out-of-scope. Surfacing these, in workshops or in definitive lists of 'out-of-scope' items as early as possible, will give the project clarity and the business greater certainty on what it can expect from the project. It may transpire that once the business realises that something that it thought was in scope turns out to be out of scope, then rather than enlarge the project, a separate project should be established to undertake this other work, taking care not to introduce any gaps or overlaps in scope. This clarification of scope can be a very valuable discovery. The more that everyone is 'on the same page' as early as possible, the better it will be for all concerned.

Clarify uncertainty – it is not unreasonable for some things to be uncertain, but what is important is that everyone – in both the business and the project – is clear on what is currently not fully known. Identifying the methods and timescales for reaching clarity would be helpful. Identifying who will undertake the clarifying activities is useful. Another key point is identifying the consequences of continuing not to know particular pieces of information. These consequences could vary over time, i.e. they may not be too much of a problem for a while, but when the project reaches a particular point in its lifecycle, the risks and therefore costs of not knowing could escalate dramatically.

It is worth defining the team boundaries, all the players and roles – even if these are not yet filled. Include the business side of the wider team.

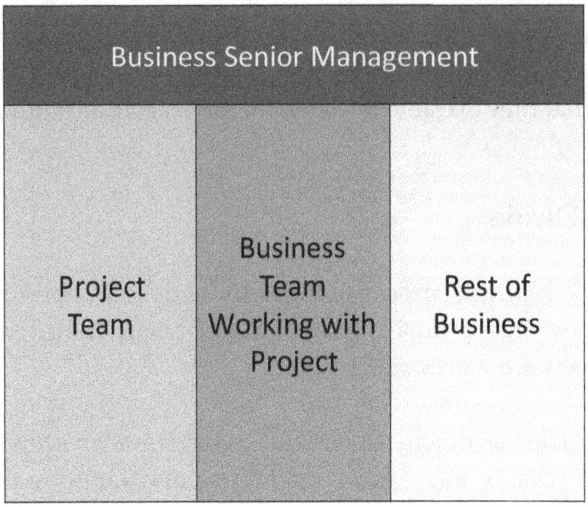

Business Senior Management		
Project Team	Business Team Working with Project	Rest of Business

Figure 2.1   Identify the teams involved

Maximum clarity of what does or does not change as a result of the project is central to making sure that everyone involved knows what the project is going to achieve.

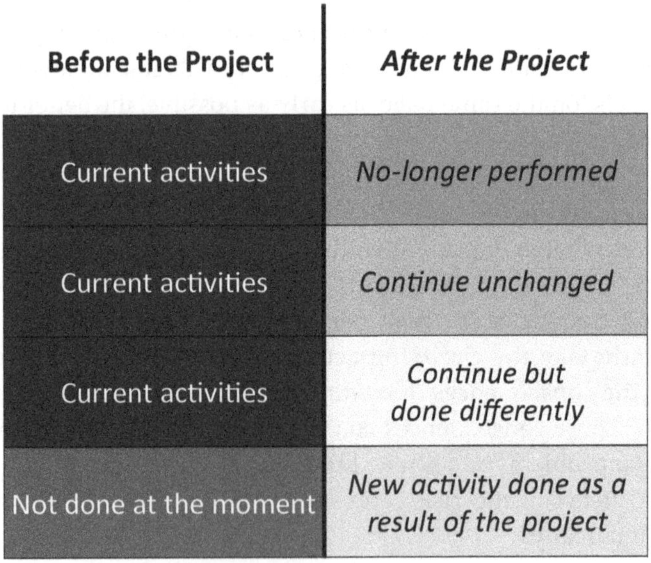

Before the Project	After the Project
Current activities	*No-longer performed*
Current activities	*Continue unchanged*
Current activities	*Continue but done differently*
Not done at the moment	*New activity done as a result of the project*

Figure 2.2   How the project changes the business

Perceptions of timing can be different; it can feel to the project team as if sometimes the business organisation seems to be suffering from a flip-flop mentality. This tends to involve a rather unpredictable switch between two opposite states: drift and panic. Neither state is conducive to an effective project, but the middle ground is sometimes hard to reach. The two parties need to find a way to discuss relative priorities. It is quite common for a day-to-day business to find that what was a 'change priority' becomes overwhelmed by emergent urgent actions, or that a gradual increase in the volume of day-to-day activity causes the 'change priority' to drift off into the in-tray labelled 'pending' and after a while to be forgotten about and in effect end up on hold, without this ever being the deliberately intended outcome.

Another aspect of timing is the concept of immovable deadlines. This book will mention this in a number of chapters, as it is the absolute bugbear for a project manager. A classic example of this is when projects are sometimes driven by acquisition or disposal timeframes which do not suit them. If the business does not understand what is entailed in a project, it can inadvertently set deadlines for a particular activity without reference to how long the project will take. The project is then presented by the business with a 'fait accompli' that forces a near-impossible timeline on to the project team. In the real world, the number of projects that actually have truly immovable deadlines is very small. Legislation can create some – if a legal obligation exists for a particular service to start on a given day, then that is in effect fixed, while major events (sporting, cultural) that run to calendar cycles are also fixed. However, most other projects can have their deadlines moved. The reasons for a timeframe choice by the business may be political (something has to be delivered before a political sponsor is next up for election) or it may be financia (the business wants something on or off its 'books' by the start of the next financial year). Alternatively, it may be reputational (the business sponsor puts their name to a date – maybe plucked out of the air – and now it is in the public domain, so face must not be lost and therefore the date must be kept to even though it is completely arbitrary). From a project perspective, the earlier that project team members are involved with the business, the more they can explain convincingly to the business what is involved and why a project needs a certain timeline, the greater the chance that they will not find themselves painted into a corner and faced with an impossible timeframe. In practice, when this happens, project teams tend to acquiesce to the deadlines they are given, knuckle-down and just work as hard as they can to deliver. This can have awful consequences for the work-life balance of the project team and the levels of stress within the team. The error and problem rates in the deliverables tend to go up as a result. A dysfunctional working environment, riven with conflict, can arise. There is a real incentive to avoid this and both business and project teams need to get together early to establish how a mature and sensibly timetabled project can be established that can still meet the aspirations of the business.

Sorting out who is in charge and who has the final say when a dispute arises can be invaluable. At a senior level in the business, there may be a number of conflicting agendas that are all driving the creation of a project, but that are focused on getting different things out of the project. Each will emphasise different aspects of what the project needs to concentrate on and will support and prioritise different actions and solutions to the challenges confronting the project. The project team could be faced with having to 'answer to many masters', which is a recipe for confusion. If the business is not used to creating the governance structures that need to sit above a project – a project board, a lead business owner, an identifiable client – then the project team may need to facilitate the establishment of these. This involves the project team crossing the boundary and entering into the business world; if done sensitively and well, this can help to cement a strong working relationship and position the project for success. Without this clarity on 'where the buck stops', when the project is faced with the inevitable problems that all projects encounter, it will not be clear where the ultimate decision-making authority rests. The project will either make a decision and then find it over-ruled, and have to reverse-out some of the work that it has done or, worse, it may find itself in indecision limbo whilst it tries to reconcile conflicting views of multiple business stakeholders without having any way of knowing for certain which set of stakeholders are the ultimate arbiters of what should be done.

Key Points

- Projects are not an end in themselves. They exist because the business wants or needs to do something differently in the future compared to how it is done today.

- Unless the business agrees that the project is needed, it will not happen.

- The project perspective on identification is focused around identifying the sponsor, the team, the scope, the deliverables, the timescales and the methods to be followed.

- The members of the project team need to gain clarity on this as soon as possible so that they are able to shape the project accordingly.

- To bridge the divide, both parties need to understand the points made above and then:

  - clarify the scope as much as possible;
  - remove and minimise uncertainty;
  - establish business and project teams and their levels of involvement;
  - be clear on what will and will not change as a result of the project;
  - confirm the level of priority for the project;
  - achieve maximum clarity of target dates, in particular which deadlines (if any) are really immovable;
  - establish who is in charge for both the project and the parts of the business sponsoring and interacting with the project.

Chapter 3

Justification and Approval
for a Project

The Business Perspective

Why do organisations want to know if something is worth doing? This could be necessary to enable the allocation of scarce resources, having to choosing between different projects and being in a position to support the evaluation of it afterwards.

Justifying and approving a project are key business activities. Some organisations have detailed processes and procedures to authorise activities and expenditure. Others may have an annual budgeting cycle, but not necessarily the framework to approve and slot a project budget into a set of regular day-in/day-out activities.

Items that the business is likely to consider include the following:

- The budget itself – size, significance relative to other projects, significance relative to day-to-day activities and what this might do to cash flow.

- The objectives of the project – how the organisation would be different once the project has delivered.

- The Return on Investment (RoI) that the project would provide for the business, or a similar financial measure such as Net Present Value (NPV).

- The urgency of the project and how it fits with other organisational priorities.

- The timeline for the project and how this dovetails with other planned projects and known changes.

- What are the peak activity periods for the business? Will these busy periods reduce the available time that business resources have for contributing to the project?

The degree to which the project is aligned with the strategy of the business will make a difference. This can vary between whether the project delivers a major strategic change, is more of an enabler that needs to be done so that a main part of the strategy can be achieved, or is actually a side-show or even a distraction from the organisation's desired direction of travel.

This overlaps with the 'want to' versus 'need to' spectrum. 'Want to' relates to ambition and strategy. 'Need to' relates to imposition – be it a government directive, a new law that needs to be complied with or a software system that is going out of support and therefore needs either upgrading or replacing. The 'need to' end of the spectrum provides a ready-made 'burning platform' which has to be jumped off, thus forcing the project to get started. The 'want to' end is more aspirational and there may be people in the organisation who do not share the ambition. A deliberate activity may be required to construct an equivalent 'burning platform' which will help to motivate the business to unite around the project.

The business may not be particularly interested in the technicalities of the delivery or any technology involved, but it is much more likely to be concerned with the project outcomes. This is often where a disconnect between the business and project worlds arises.

The Project Perspective

The project perspective on project justification and approval tends to focus on establishing the project as a distinct entity. It will need funding, which may come in the form of a purchase order if the project is undertaken by a team that is external to the business.

Key items that the project will want include the following.

- Terms of Reference.

- Mandate – sometimes a specific document. Many methods provide 'template' documents for these purposes.

- Budget for the project – including items such as team costs, accommodation, tools, input materials and suppliers. This may be a subset of the overall costs, as business members who shadow the project may not be costed as part of the project team. This can lead to confusion and disagreements later when it becomes clear that different players made different assumptions about whether a project was picking up certain sets of costs or whether they fall to the business unit where the resource resides. This might be costs of the shadow team member and/or costs of a backfill resource.

- The time dimension for the project budget needs clarity. If it is multi-year, has the budget been granted for the whole project or does new funding need to be approved and allocated when the next financial year arrives?

Talking about time, the realism of the timeline and schedule for the project will form a key aspect of the justification for the project team. A set of costs for the project, based on estimated effort and duration, will be driven by what needs to be delivered by when, and therefore what resources are required to deliver it. As part of the definition, the project will want to build in contingency in the form of time and resources. The degree of novelty and challenge associated with the project, together with the project team's level of confidence about being able to deliver to the estimated schedule, will affect the amount of contingency.

If there is a commercial relationship between the project and the business, then the approach taken in relation to contingency will be more complex. With two separate organisations – a customer and a supplier – there is a possibility that if unforeseen events affect the amount of effort and time taken to deliver the project, one or other party might suffer financially. The two main types of commercial arrangement have different features:

- In a Time and Materials (T&M) project, the supplier is paid for all of the work they do and all of the material they provide, irrespective of whether this is more than might have been estimated originally. This can expose the customer (i.e. the business) to greater costs than they were expecting and can make what might have seemed like an economic project no longer appear to be worth doing. The customer may set aside some contingency in their budget to cover such a situation.

- In a fixed-price project, the supplier is paid an agreed amount. If the supplier takes longer than expected or uses more staff than planned, they still receive the amount originally agreed. This gives the customer certainty that the amount they will spend on the project is fixed, but can expose the supplier to the risk of financial loss. This means that at the start, when the supplier is working out the fixed price of the project, they are likely to include an allowance for contingency so that if something does go wrong, they will not make a loss.

In effect, for a given deliverable under a fixed-price arrangement, the customer is potentially paying more for a given deliverable than under a T&M arrangement that goes to plan, but is protected from the risk of having to pay any more than the fixed price.

In rare cases, there is a more sophisticated approach of a shared risk-reward, with additional incentive payments being made for meeting or beating agreed timelines. This will result in an approach to contingency that reflects these arrangements.

Bridging the Divide

To bridge the divide between the teams at this stage and to lay the groundwork to prevent a division arising later, a number of points need consideration.

First is the 'realise-ability' of the benefits. In reality, are the benefits achievable? Will this happen almost automatically as a byproduct of the project's deliverables being provided or will substantial effort – including by the business – be required?

It is important to make sure that there is no mismatch of timelines. Consider the annual business cycles and the fit with strategic three- or five-year plans. How long will the project take and how will this overlay these business cycles? Consider the ability of the business' annual expenditure budgets to cope with an acceleration or a delay in the project schedule.

Are there other external cycles that drive, divert or maybe force the pace of the project – such as a political deadline where a project has to be completed within its elected political sponsor's term of office? If the time needed to deliver the project is seriously at variance with the available political time, then early frank conversations relating to adjusting the scope or the timeline will be required.

Agreed positions and clarity on what efficiency savings the project will deliver (if it is that type of project) will help. Being able to do a task more quickly will not necessarily lead to savings in terms of staff costs if there are other activities that staff could be doing and have postponed until now. The organisation could end up delivering more but retaining the same level of costs – which ought not to come as a surprise. Getting these assumptions out in the open is key to having everyone on the same page.

A tricky area is where an organisation is too optimistic about a project. To get funding approval, it takes a best-case approach so that work can get started. However, it soon comes to light that there is much more work involved and that the most likely outcome will be closer to the worst-case option in the original business case. Once started, projects tend to be quite hard to stop – a lot of people quickly end up with prestige invested and do not want to be associated with something that was stopped midway and did not complete. Projects can therefore be at risk from unrealistic low early estimates which get the activity started, only to find that their costs and timescales soon spiral out of control.

Pragmatism is an element of an effective joint justification process. A balance will sometimes need to be struck in terms of how much effort is expended on the justification activity. On occasions, organisations just do not have quantified data about how much time and cost are involved in their current processes. A decision needs to be made about the cost of working out these costs and factoring that into the cost of making a decision about whether to go ahead with a project.

Key Points

- A project is often only one of a number of competing demands on a business for scarce resources.

- In order to make an informed decision on whether to go ahead with a project, the case for the project needs to be put in business language that enables easy comparisons between it and the other areas and activities which could also use the money that the project would need.

- Businesses sometimes have projects they need to do – e.g. government directives or out-of-date technology that needs upgrading – that have to take priority over projects that they want to do in support of implementing a new business strategy.

- 'Need to do' projects are often easier to get going than 'want to do' projects because the former cannot be ignored, whilst the latter will need the business to motivate itself to get started.

- The business may not be particularly interested in the technicalities of the delivery or any technology involved, but it is much more likely to be concerned with the project outcomes.

- The project view on justification focuses on establishing approved funding – sometimes a purchase order to a separate organisation – for the project team to be created.

- To enable justification, the project will need to agree the deliverables and also the time schedule for the project.

- Where a project is subcontracted, there is an interplay between who takes the risk of the project going wrong and how the project is priced. In a fixed-price arrangement that includes risk contingency in the price, the customer is potentially paying more for a given deliverable than under a T&M arrangement that goes to plan. However, the customer is protected from the risk of having to pay any more than the fixed price.

- To bridge the divide, both parties need to understand the points made above and then:

    – invest time and effort upfront to reduce the chances of conflict later;
    – agree how the business will gain benefit from the project's deliverables and to what extent the project team will need to be involved in realising the benefits;
    – confirm how the project schedule and the regular pattern of business activities can be best fitted together;

- understand whether arbitrary deadlines, set by high-level sponsors, are really achievable and what might need to be done if it is discovered later on that they are impossible to meet;
- start to get assumptions surfaced, documented and agreed;
- form a joint view on whether the timeline for the project is realistic or over-optimistic;
- be pragmatic with the justification process. There will be unknowns and surprises, so trying to identify and account for every last detail of a potential project will lead to it spending too long in the justification phase.

Chapter 4
Getting Started

The Business Perspective

To the business, the activities involved in getting a project started can seem like excessive slow bureaucracy. Most tasks involved in the day-to-day running of an organisation can be started or ramped-up relatively simply. A line manager can re-assign a member of their team to a new task, adjust their regular schedule or request a bit of overtime. This means that an expectation exists that things will happen quickly and with minimum hassle. Projects do not follow this pattern, but business staff may not fully appreciate how different they are in terms of getting started. This can easily manifest itself in business impatience and early disillusionment: 'Why haven't we started yet?'

The role of the business within a project may not be evident to members of the business. They are likely to have a set of requirements, which, having engaged a project manager to deliver, they will then put on to the 'back-burner' in terms of their own priorities. But the project as it starts to come into existence will make demands upon the business that may be unexpected. The business participants find themselves asking the following questions:

- 'Why do I have to come to all these extra meetings?'

- 'What is this new project role I've just been lumbered with? I already have a day job'.

- 'Where has this large crowd of people just come from?'

The business has got up a head of steam and is enthusiastic for the project to get underway and make visible progress. In fact, the sooner the deliverables can be given to the business, the better. From a business perspective, the tasks involved in setting up the project can appear to be very convoluted and nit-picky.

The key difference here is that the business already exists in terms of its structure, organisation and support functions. All the people are in place, they have job titles and roles, they know each other and they know what each other do. What they do is fairly predictable as it follows a regular pattern of activity – be it daily, weekly or monthly. Everyone is already equipped with office space and the technology they need to do their jobs, and they exist on the HR system and the payroll system. They have objectives and personal development plans. And, having worked together for a while, they function as a team – more or less.

Clearly the effectiveness of team working will vary between business teams, but the central point is that they have developed a collective modus operandi. If someone is away, it is quite likely that another team member can step into their shoes and cover for them, and the resulting work will be of reasonable quality. Everyone has already climbed their learning curve, which has happened gradually over a period of time. The function may have been in existence for many years, even if it is more recent; nonetheless, in all cases it will have evolved slowly. The tasks needed to set it up – staff onboarding, job roles, inductions, plans, team bonding, performance monitoring and tracking Key Performance Indicators – all of these will have been added into the mix by a process of accretion. This is where a project is fundamentally different. And this is why there can be a disconnect at this stage in a project's lifecycle.

The Project Perspective

More often than not, projects start with nothing. They may make use of some in-house staff if there is a function in the organisation that does the type of project that is needed, but even this may not be the case.

A project that starts from scratch has to boot itself up whilst at the same time starting to get on with the activities related to providing deliverables to the business. Getting started covers a number of areas and involves answering and taking action related to a number of key questions:

- What are we delivering?

- How are we going to deliver it?

- How much time have we got available to do this delivery?

- Is what we are being asked to provide buildable – in principle and more specifically in the available time?

- Who is going to do the delivery?

- What environment, tools and infrastructure do we need?

- How can we get hold of the people and equipment we need to do the job?

A fortunate project has time to find answers to these questions, take action and then get started on the main delivery. A project that is subject to tight time pressures may need to undertake the delivery tasks whilst still stumbling into existence.

Let us get back to these key questions for a moment. The justification activity that preceded the getting-started activity may have provided partial answers to some of these questions. This will vary depending upon how extensive and thorough the justification process was. If the project was subject to rigorous early analysis, then the answers will already exist and the task will simply be to put the identified actions into play. However, if the justification process was less extensive or simply consisted of a barked order of 'Just get on with it' emanating from somewhere on high, then the project manager will need to consider these points in detail before the project will have been established with a firm foundation.

WHAT ARE WE DELIVERING?

This may seem startlingly obvious to the business, particularly sponsors and people paying for the project. In fact, this is where the bane of unconfirmed assumptions can first come into play. What is needed is a clear specification of the deliverables, covering all the relevant categories, which can include physical objects (sometimes known as the core deliverables, e.g. a building, a road, a new product or a computer) but also all the other deliverables (which can range across documents, organisational changes – including the hiring or departure of people – the acquisition or disposal of companies and changes to the way in which an organisation works), new processes, training in those processes and general cultural change to ensure that the rest of the project is successful. This is where the assumptions trap comes into play for the first time, as the business and the project may well have quite different presumptions about what does or does not constitute a deliverable from the project. 'What's the point of a new system if we don't have the staff trained and enthusiastically lined up to use it?' might be the business viewpoint; to which the project could answer: 'But you only asked for the system, there was nothing in the Terms of Reference relating to training the staff'. This is why a complete and unambiguous definition of what is to be delivered is required.

There are also nuances within this that need to be taken into account. One relates to what is not yet known. It is a classic in modern management speak that there are often aspects of a situation that are not known. These themselves can be divided down into those that people are aware that they do not yet know (e.g. we will have to get rid of people but do not yet know if it will be 20 or 200) and aspects that the people did not realise they did not know. A project is rarely in the lucky position to be able to get started knowing everything. Most of the time there are aspects of what is to be delivered – and how best to deliver it – that are uncertain when things are getting started. There is an interplay here with assumptions. The business may assume that the project realises that some aspects of the deliverables are uncertain, while similarly the project may assume that the business realises that some aspects of how the project is going to be delivered are not yet known. In both cases this may not be the case, and the unknown deliverables and the unknown project processes emerge later during the lifecycle as a nasty surprise for all concerned. Why a nasty surprise? Because by the time they emerge, the project has moved on to the extent that such surprises will disrupt the timeline and cost considerably more to change direction and incorporate these newly discovered aspects than would have been the case if they had been considered in the plan from the start. So to tackle this, the assumptions need to be brought out blinking into the daylight. The classic approach to this, which is perfectly adequate in the vast majority of cases, is via one or more joint workshops where the project and business come together, step back from the day-to-day tasks of the project set-up and via a facilitator highlight all the things that they assumed that the other party had already realised. Once identified, the assumptions should all be documented in a Register which can be made available across the project and the business so that all parties are aware of what is being assumed. In a few cases where there are two opposite assumptions (business assumes project is doing X, while project assumes it is not doing X and that X is the sole responsibility of the business), this may actually lead to the assumption being converted into a new part of the business-project agreement whereby a shared view is established on what is to be done by whom and the ambiguity and uncertainty is removed.

Another nuance relates to scope and boundaries. Even if there is clarity on what could be called the 'central deliverables', i.e. you are delivering a new system, there may be ambiguity in terms of what this includes on the edges. If the computer system has to work with other systems, then there may be a need for interfaces to be developed and provided. Different parties may make opposite assumptions about whether these fall within the scope of the project – traditionally the business will assume that they are included, as they would expect to get everything they need to make the system work, whereas the project would assume that unless they are explicitly stated as a deliverable, then they would not be automatically included as part of the project. Again, working through the assumptions, via workshops, and capturing these in a shared, documented and widely distributed Assumptions Register will help to reduce this potential problem.

One caveat about the Assumptions Register is that some parts of the organisation may be less used to working with uncertainties. Such individuals will, for perfectly understandable reasons, tend to treat the statements in the Assumptions Register as facts. If these later turn out to be invalid assumptions, with significant consequences for the project, then recriminations may ensue. To avoid this, the provisional nature of the statements in the Assumptions Register should be emphasised when it is distributed to a wider audience.

FIRM SCOPE AND REALISTIC ESTIMATES

There is one other area which can lead to confusion in terms of what is going to be delivered. This can arise when the project is being undertaken by a team from a distinct and separate business from the client business. In this situation, the project may well have needed to be sold by the project provider to the business. This sales process tends to be done by sales specialists, who are expert in finding opportunities and clarifying customer requirements, responding to complex requests for proposals or invitations to tender, and can then navigate the tortuous process of 'closing the deal' and getting the customer to sign of the dotted line and contractually agree that the provider organisation will be the one that undertakes the project. These teams are very good at what they do, but quite often what they do does not include the details of laying the groundwork for the set-up of the project that has been sold. They tend to be distinct and separate from the delivery team, and, due to commitments to other projects, members of the new project team may have had very limited visibility of the sales process that has led to the award of the project.

To address this concern and risk, a proper handover is needed from any sales/bid/proposal team across to the project team. The scenario to avoid is one of 'we won it, now you deliver it...'. This disconnect can lead to a very big risk if the sales team are so focused on winning the business that they do so at the expense of it actually being deliverable. This can be the start of the 'over-promise and under-deliver' nightmare. To avoid this fully, the project team needs to be involved in the sales process to an adequate extent to provide some 'governance input' around whether what is being proposed, as well as looking good, is something that can actually be delivered. This involvement needs to happen, in a light-touch way, all through the sales activity. Provided this has happened and a realistic project has been submitted and then won, the second step is to ensure a full and detailed handover from the sales team to the project team. This can best be illustrated by defining the opposite. The behaviour that most needs to be avoided is one of 'throwing it over the wall' with the sales team rapidly melting into the mist and disappearing the moment the project has been won, leaving the newly forming project delivery team to pick up the pieces before the project has even started. The much-preferred scenario is where the sales team provides a full set of documentation and a diary audit trail of how the sales process went, a stakeholder map of the client's key players (including their expectations) and actually facilitates personal introductions of the project team to the business so that it is clear that a mature and complete internal handover from the sales team to the project team has occurred. There is no harm in doing this very visibly in front of the business, as this should give the business increased confidence that the aspirations they have shared with the sales part of the project delivery organisation have been passed across to the project delivery team, and that they are acknowledged, understood and will be reflected in the way in which the project is set up and run. In fact, the business should be concerned if it does not see evidence that this has happened; it may wish to actively push for a demonstrable handover to occur.

HOW ARE WE GOING TO DELIVER IT?

This may seem obvious, but in practice considerable thought may be required in order to identify the right set of 'ways of working'. The focus of this covers the methods and processes that the project is going to follow. These fall into a number of categories. Some are more abstract in that they relate to how a project is run irrespective of what the project is delivering, while others are specific to the type of project.

All projects need a list of what they are going to produce, a timeline or plan for what tasks are going to happen when, a way of dealing with changes, a way of making sure that the deliverables are of the right quality and a way of reporting progress and alerting senior management to problems. This can be provided by following a recognised method such as PRINCE2® (TSO for

AXELOS 2009) or the approaches published by the Association for Project Management (APM 2013) or the Project Management Institute (PMI 2013).

Other aspects are much more specific to the type of project. Building a bridge, implementing a computer system, re-organising a department – all of these can be done using a project. The tasks that need to be done will differ greatly in terms of what needs to be performed in order to create a physical structure or an electronic artefact or a differently structured team of people.

This is where a project, when it starts up, needs to determine how it will go about creating its deliverables. Some projects may have ready access to a set of processes and methods, as they are housed in a function, or delivered by an organisation that specialises in projects and therefore has an 'off-the-shelf' method that can be adjusted to suit the needs of the particular project. Other projects, which exist with less of a support structure, will first need to invest time and effort in determining what are the right methods and processes for them to follow. This can be tricky to explain to the business as it appears that no actual 'real work' is being done, but without this first step, the project will get off to a very uncertain start and will proceed in a haphazard fashion.

HOW MUCH TIME HAVE WE GOT AVAILABLE TO DO THIS DELIVERY?

This may or may not be at the discretion of the project itself. In some cases the business in dialogue with the project will ask the project for an estimate of how long the project is expected to take. Where this happens, the project needs to develop a detailed enough plan to be able to identify all the substantial tasks involved, how they all fit together in sequence, whether some can be done at the same time and, when they are all put together into a single plan, how long the overall project will take.

The project itself may vary in the degree of confidence it has in its own estimate. If many similar tasks have been undertaken before, ideally by the same team, then their knowledge of how long it took to do the previous projects, and their individual tasks, can inform an evidence-based estimate for this project. However, if the project is novel, uses new techniques or uses staff who are not particularly experienced in their planned roles, then the resulting estimated duration is less likely to match the eventual out-turn.

The project can make a trade-off here with regard to how much detail it includes in the plan. The greater the level of detail, the better the chances that the estimate will be realistic. This is because more tasks will have been identified and the time for each task will have been considered separately. A higher-level sketchier plan is more likely to include assumptions that may turn out not to be warranted and thus trip up the project, resulting in a different duration from that expected.

IS WHAT WE ARE BEING ASKED TO PROVIDE BUILDABLE?

This is a key question that the project will want to ask before getting started. The business will presume that the requested project is achievable. A good project will include a degree of scepticism and will challenge this assumption. It is better to uncover potential problems and pitfalls earlier rather than when the project is well advanced. This is not for reasons of pessimism, but actually to give confidence that the plan is well-founded and that the project can safely move forward.

It is worth noting that having determined that a project is buildable, there is a different question that should also be asked, which is whether the project is worth building. This will be considered later in this book in Chapter 16.

The handover issue mentioned earlier can also affect whether a set of deliverables are buildable. This particular challenge can come when the project has been designed, sold and won by one team (the sales team) and then passed on to a separate team to undertake the project (the delivery team). The members of the project team may suddenly find themselves with a set of delivery obligations which they did not have any part in creating or agreeing to. In the worst-case scenario, they can feel 'stitched up', with an obligation to provide something that, although it appeared fine when it was being sold, turns out to be much harder to build than the sales team expected. This can prompt and justify a legitimate scrutiny of what has just landed on the doormat in order to make sure that what the project team is about to take on can actually be done.

There is also a secondary question that a good project will ask. Having determined that what is being requested can be built, it then needs to check if it can be built in the available time. The project may have a timeframe and deadline that are outside the control of the project team. Although the required deliverables could be created, their complexities, interdependencies, the supply chain, the necessary raw materials, the skills required from the team and the resources needed simply may not be available in suitable quantities or quickly enough to enable the deliverables to be achieved in the available time.

Again, although this may appear negative, it is actually a very important part of the project's due diligence. By determining this upfront and alerting the business to this problem right from the start, a negotiation process can be entered into to resolve the problem. It might be possible to deliver half the project, to provide all the deliverables, but to only half the planned locations, to renegotiate the timeline and extend the project or to remove a resource constraint by increasing the budget. It is better that this surfaces earlier, because the longer a project waits to share this type of bad news with the business, the nastier the surprise will be for everyone, the less remaining time there will be to find a remedy and the more it will cost to resolve.

WHO IS GOING TO DO THE DELIVERY?

This question may seem obvious, but the project will need to design its organisation structure based on the tasks that it has to perform in order to create the deliverables it is being asked to provide. Default roles may exist, such as Project Manager, Assurance Manager, Project Office Manager, Designer, Developer and Tester, but these then need to be brought together into an organisational framework that is specific to this project.

The quantities of resource also need to be determined. There may be only one Project Manager, but how many designers and testers are required? Also, 'When are they needed?', since not all activities will start at once or last for the

Month 1	Month 2	Month 3	Month 4	Month 5	Month 6	Month 7
				Junior Developer		
			Junior Developer	Junior Developer		
			Junior Developer	Lead Developer	Lead Developer	
			Lead Developer	Junior Tester	Junior Tester	Handover Manager
		Junior Designer	Junior Designer	Senior Tester	Senior Tester	Senior Tester
		Senior Designer	Senior Designer	Senior Designer	Senior Designer	Senior Designer
	PO Manager	PO Manager	PO Manager	PO Manager	PO Manager	PO Manager
	Assurance Manager	Assurance Manager	Assurance Manager	Assurance Manager	Assurance Manager	Assurance Manager
Project Manager	Project Manager	Project Manager	Project Manager	Project Manager	Project Manager	Project Manager

Table 4.1   Pattern of staffing during a project

full duration of the project. The team needs to be planned fully, including its growth and shrinkage over time as the project progresses. At the end of this activity, there will not yet be an active project, simply a degree of clarity on what roles are needed, how many, when from and for how long. This is the start of the project's HR plan of action.

WHAT ENVIRONMENT, TOOLS AND INFRASTRUCTURE DO WE NEED?

Other logistical elements can also affect how quickly the team can come up to speed. A project is an organisation in itself, there may be a need to provide a range of equipment (suitably configured laptops), office space, shared storage for online documents, security clearances for team members or the field next to the road being widened to hold the site office. None of these is difficult in itself, but there tend to be assumptions that they can be provided instantly and in quite large volumes by the host organisation. This is rarely the case, so often new project team members are faced with a poorly organised start and induction (sometimes known in the jargon as onboarding) into the team.

The project as a 'mini-organisation' also has to sort out various other aspects of its own housekeeping. This will include activities such as project finances, timesheets, expenditure tracking and matching against client payments. There may be a suite of systems and tools (very often complex spreadsheets) that enable this, but even so, this all needs to be put in place and kicked off. Similarly, HR arrangements for the team members need to be established and steps taken to build a shared vision and team spirit for the project.

HOW CAN WE GET HOLD OF THE PEOPLE AND EQUIPMENT WE NEED TO DO THE JOB?

This is all about ramping up the team. Having a 'standing army' costs a lot, so most organisations will not have a spare set of project resources in place that can all start working on day one. It can take time to find them, particularly the right people. In fact there is a natural limit to the rate at which new team members can be onboarded. Too many joining at the same time will divert the flow of the project from making progress into simply assimilating all the new staff onto the team. A project needs an *esprit de corps* and this is often best fostered by growing the team incrementally. Too many staff arriving at the same time can lead to confusion and lack of direction, as well as overstretch for the existing team members who need to devote effort to inducting the new members.

However, once in place, a 'marching army' also costs money. Project staff need to be productive and it is not good to have them waiting around to get started. A team of designers who cannot get started producing the detailed design because the requirements have not yet been agreed with the business will cause problems. To keep them busy, a design may be put together but based on a large number of assumptions, and it will need extensive rework once the requirements have been finalised. In addition, delays such as this can impact morale and set a bad tone early in the project.

Bridging the Divide

This may all feel excessive to the business, but what is key to understand is that without a firm foundation, the project will simply be a house built on sand. It is important to get the details correct right at the start. Something small that is neglected or done badly in the set-up, although seeming minor, can have an effect that is multiplied considerably downstream and will potentially have a much greater negative impact on the project than might be expected. An Internet search for the proverb 'For Want of a Nail' will give a feel for the sort of consequences that can arise from a small item being overlooked at the start of an endeavour.

So how do we attempt to bridge this gap at the project start-up? Remember, this is key because an early disconnect can itself grow into mutual incomprehension and deep mistrust if a strong business-project link is not established. What do we need to consider and take action about?

JOINT TEAMING

This involves bringing the project personnel and the business staff who are on the edge of the project together into a single unified team. At a tactical level, fusing them into one team means they should be united and concentrate on tackling external challenges rather than splitting into two camps that do not know or understand each other and thus focus their efforts on blaming and fighting each other.

The classic concept of Tuckman team stages (Tuckman 1965) will naturally apply to this activity. The concepts relating to these stages of evolution of team performance going through Forming, Storming, Norming, Performing and Mourning are generally well established within both the business and project worlds. The critical point to take on board here is that because the team will grow incrementally, it will go through multiple parallel strands of these stages. An assumption by the early joiners that the first few stages have been achieved and performing reached will turn out to be undermined if additional new joiners are not actively engaged into the team.

Initial team	F	S	N	P	P	P	P	P
Second group		F	S	N	P	P	P	P
Third group			F	S	N	P	P	P

F = Forming / S = Storming / N = Norming / P = Performing

Table 4.2   Impact of new joiners on team performance

BUSINESS IMPACT

The benefits to the project of including members of the business in a unified team will be lost if a number of hygiene factors are not addressed. It is important to properly sort out the secondment of the business team members so that they have clarity about what is expected of them, which may differ significantly from their day jobs. They are likely to be included in the project for their business knowledge, but not necessarily for the operational skills they use on a day-to-day basis. They will need inducting into the project and to receive training on how to be effective project team members. Care must also be taken with backfilling the roles of the seconded staff. This is central to ensuring that the business team members are not overloaded from their old day job, with a leakage of time, effort, energy and focus back to the business. This leakage can take a number of forms – one is where, whilst they are on the project as the 'resident expert' in their area, their time and knowledge is repeated requested by the business because they are best placed to resolve tricky day-to-day problems faced by the business. The other form of leakage is simply related to not having someone to take over the day job, which means that the business team member ends up doing two jobs – the new one on the project and the old day-to-day one. Finding backfill resources can take time and projects tend to march off into the distance regardless of the degree to which the business resources are available and ready to help.

BUSINESS TEAM TRAINING

One area of risk to project success is unwarranted assumptions. A classic example of this is assuming that all members of the business team are familiar with and understand the way that projects work. It is well worth checking whether this is actually the case. Of course, levels of project familiarity may vary. In particular, senior management and junior team members may be less project aware than middle management, who could well have participated in projects before. Sensitivity is needed here so as not to be perceived as being patronising to business team members who do understand projects. An appropriate sounding-out of the key players in order to get an understanding of how familiar team members are is a good first step. On the basis of this, the project team may well need to brief and, if necessary, train some the business members in the lifecycle and techniques being used by the project. As part of this induction, it is well worth explaining why the various types of paperwork and apparent bureaucracy are needed, what benefit they bring, the risks of ignoring or skimping on them, and the active role that the business team needs to play. When one is familiar with a particular activity or process, the documentation involved in it can seem both reasonable and necessary; when one is unfamiliar, the same level of documentation can seem daunting and excessive. There is no 'one-size-fits-all' approach to this, and the same consideration about new joiners arriving during the ramp-up of the project applies again as it did earlier. This means that the induction material can usefully be codified into a set of briefing notes and training material that can be repeatedly delivered as and when new business team members arrive.

RECIPROCAL INDUCTION

At the same time as getting the business team up to speed with the working concepts and methods of the project, it is also valuable to focus on the project team. In this case the aim is to make a point of inducting the project team members into the business team's world. The project team may not be particularly familiar with the business. This could encompass the core business of the organisation, how it is structured, how performance is measured and what the working pattern and calendar is for the business. All of these unwritten norms provide a context that the business team will be familiar with, but one that can trip up the project team members. Time spent on such an induction can be more than paid back as the project team members will then appreciate the subtleties of the way in which the business works and will finesse their approach to make sure that the project runs smoothly within the context provided by the business.

Whilst considering induction, it is worth noting that there may be 'business as usual' processes that support some of the onboarding and housekeeping functions; however, because the project team may all be new, they may not be aware of them. Project induction should therefore start with the Project Manager and should include an introduction to the support systems – human, logistical and technological – provided by the host organisation.

Induction activities should be repeated regularly as the teams grow. Do not just focus on the first few joiners and then expect everyone else to pick things up by osmosis – deliberately make sure that all those joining the project and shadow business teams get a full induction.

HEARTBEAT

Projects run to a pattern of activities that is separate from the main business. The phased nature of project activities can feel alien to someone who is used to a regular routine of work pattern. However, the control mechanisms of a project do tend to run to a calendar of some sort. This is when the heartbeat of the project is established. They consist of the obvious (to the project team) regularly monthly and weekly meetings and reporting cycles. An indication of the intensity and pace of the project is often the frequency of such meetings. A project that is running to schedule and not facing too many challenges may choose to operate monthly senior management meetings and weekly team meetings and reporting. If things are not going well, even from the start, then the frequency can be adjusted to weekly senior level meetings and daily progress meetings. These often happen at the start of a day and can be known in some organisations as 'morning prayers'. The advent of ubiquitous conference-call technology can mean that once a team has gelled with face-to-face meetings for the first few days, these often turn into teleconferences. However the heartbeat is established, what matters is to get business members of the team involved from the start.

AGREEMENTS

The effective use of agreements can provide a very good mechanism to achieve bridge building. The nature of the project–business relationship will drive the type of agreements that are developed. If the project is being provided by a totally separate organisation, then inevitably there will be a legal contract between the project's organisation and the business organisation. The trick here is to cover all eventualities from a legal perspective, which trained lawyers are expert at doing, but in a way that enables flexibility to be achieved. The essence of a contract is that it should provide clarity about what is to be delivered, how success will be judged and how one party will pay the other party. However, it is written from a pessimistic frame of mind and includes many sections that cover all the different eventualities that might go wrong. This means that 'all the bases are covered', but, as a result, the contract tends to be long, sometimes obscure and inaccessible, and generally has a negative tone. In essence, it should only be needed if something bad happens. The positive aspects, i.e. what is to be delivered, should be at the 'front and centre' of everyone's minds so that reference to the contract to check what is to be delivered should not be necessary.

As a result, one way of looking at a contract is to contrast an effective project with a troubled one. A healthy project puts the contract away in the drawer on day one, merges into one team and just gets on with it, in a spirit of cooperation, joint working and shared success. A toxic project keeps thick bound copies of the contract on the desk, refers to it every day and uses it as a brick with which to beat the other party into submission.

It is also worth noting that this contractual situation can repeat itself a number of times if the project organisation itself has suppliers who are separate organisations. Then the project needs to make sure that any obligations it takes on are flowed down to its suppliers using back-to-back contracts, which means that the supplier to the project team has the equivalent obligations and responsibilities as the project team to the business. Setting up this supply chain of contracts can take time and can delay the effective start-up of the project, particularly if there are a number of suppliers or a long chain of sub-suppliers.

Having covered the situation where there are two or more separate legal entities involved, we can now cover the other situation where both the business and the project team reside within the same organisation. Oddly enough, although one might think that this would be simpler, there is in fact greater scope for ambiguity. The reason for this is that since both the project and the business reside in the same organisation, the nature of the relationship between them is actually more informal. It is certainly unlikely to be documented in a formal contract. There may be some sort of Terms of Reference or internal Memorandum of Understanding, but in general there will not be a formal document that describes the obligations that each party has towards the other. As a result, although there may be an enumeration of what is to be delivered, the other areas that a contract addresses will not be covered in any particular document. There will be silence and presumption around the ways in which the two teams interact.

This means that instead there will need to be a fairly detailed document that gets the project started. The classic example is the Project Initiation

Document (PID) (Managing Successful Projects with PRINCE2™ 2009: 254). Whatever the title of document is, the main point is that as well as describing the deliverables and scope of supply, it also needs to address the processes and methods that the two teams (the business and the project) will use for working together. It should cover the different roles that exist in each party, what they are responsible for and in particular how they interact. It will also need to cover the governance structure – the committees and meetings which happen on a regular basis – that control how the business and project work together to steer the project forwards.

AVOIDING HISTORIC ENMITIES

An extra challenge in this situation may arise if the project and the business teams have worked together before on other projects that have not gone well. There may, as a result, be deep-seated misgivings, animosities and distrust that sit below the surface of the day-to-day conversations involved in setting up this new project. Care will need to be taken if there is such a history, as two aspects need consideration. The first relates to being clear on what went wrong on the earlier project and taking deliberate and visible action to make sure that such mistakes are not repeated. A lessons learnt workshop would be valuable. Even if one was held for the previous project, a follow-up workshop with a focus on 'How will we apply the lessons learnt from the previous project' will be valuable. The second aspect relates to the softer interpersonal issues, active steps will need to be taken to acknowledge any simmering tensions or resentments due to the earlier project and to take steps to defuse these. A project where one or both parties starts up with a view of 'I don't want to work that bunch of ...' is doomed to run into some sort of trouble sooner rather than later. This is where social activities which bring the two teams together away from the work environment can help, but a single event is unlikely to be enough. Barriers of mistrust take time to break down. Sometimes an artificial training environment, which puts the members of both parties together into a single team, to tackle some sort of challenge – maybe of a sporting or adventure nature – can help. The key here is that both parties need to become a single team, and this can be achieved by uniting them to face a common challenge and putting them in a situation where they have to rely on each other, and in doing so discover that the other party is not so bad after all. The exact activity is less important than achieving the objective of unifying the two parties into a single team so that they have more recent shared positive experiences of working together successfully that will 'over-write' in their memories the pain of the previous unsuccessful project.

STAKEHOLDER MANAGEMENT

Start-up provides the point at which Stakeholder Management needs to be developed and put into effect. This will involve analysing and classifying all of the different stakeholder groups and assigning them to appropriate categories, usually on the basis of their degree of interest and degree of influence or power (Slack et al. 2012). This has three benefits:

- it makes sure that all parts of the wider business are identified and taken into account;

- it enables the communications with each of these groups to be developed and tailored to their level of knowledge and interest in the project; and

- it provides a mechanism for prioritisation of stakeholder management activities so that a limited budget of time and effort can be deployed to the best effect.

So as not to antagonise stakeholder groups, especially if they stumble upon a stakeholder map in which they feature and about which they know nothing, it is best to be open about the stakeholder management activity. To do this, it can be very helpful if the project team enlists the help, knowledge and insights of the business team.

TIMELINE ALIGNMENT

This is also the point in time to recheck and reconfirm the alignment of the project timeline and the business' regular cycles. It is important to identify and take into consideration any potential clashes between the project timeline, particularly major events like approvals of key documents, involvement of the business in testing and acceptance, and actual 'go live' activities, and the Business as Usual calendars of regular meetings, month-end processing deadlines and predictable seasonal busy periods. This can uncover potential considerations such as 'We can't decide this now', 'We can't confirm that until then…', 'We can't change this on that date' and 'We can only go live in those two weeks, not at any other time…'. It is far better to identify these now and make the necessary amendments to the proposed project schedule than it would be to discover these later and then attempt either to ram in the project regardless or to have to make emergency re-plans to take account of these events that were foreseeable but were not identified early enough.

TEAM ASSEMBLY

Bringing the individual teams together is not as obvious as it might seem. If too many new joiners all start at the same time, then there will not be enough bandwidth to concentrate on the project. In addition, there will not be enough informed team members to provide a comprehensive and coherent introduction to the project. This may well come as a surprise to the business. Therefore, it is best to agree a way to balance everyone's strong ambition to make progress against having a realistic view on the achievable ramp-up rate for staff to join the project team.

Geography also needs to be taken into account. A project where the client business team and the project team are all in the same office is simple and straightforward. However, except perhaps for in-house IT departments, this is rarely the case these days. The split can come in one of two ways. First is a business-project split, where the business and project teams are located separately. If this is on different floors in the same building, then this is relatively trivial, but any greater degree of separation is enough to make it necessary to engage in an active effort to prevent a 'them-and-us' mentality developing by accident. Nearby buildings will still allow for regular face-to-face interchanges between the people in the teams. This should be encouraged. Although email provides an audit trail of potential agreements, at the same time it removes many of the nuances of effective communication and should be used appropriately and not just as a blanket default communication mechanism. Any greater geographical separation between the project and the business – different cities and particularly different countries (potentially exacerbated by different time zones) – should be actively countered. This can be done by deliberately choosing to hold a number of initial face-to-face meetings in the same room in order to create *esprit de corps*. Only once these relationships have been strongly established should the project and business fall back onto video and audio conferencing. The use of email only should be avoiding wherever possible as this will inevitably lead to potential misunderstandings.

We also need to consider the individual teams, particularly the project team, but also maybe the business team if this is being formed especially for the project. If the team needs to be geographically spread itself, then there is an approach that may help. Spreading a team that has previously worked together in one location around the across multiple locations will be more efficient than having separate teams who have not worked together before. This means that if it is possible to construct the team using a number of people who have worked together before in the same location, then a set of norms and effective operating practices will already exist. These are more likely to be maintained when this set of individuals is then spread around a number of locations when compared to a situation in which people who have not worked together before have to build working relationships from scratch whilst being at opposite ends of a telephone line or email exchange.

There are further considerations when the project team is itself not from a single organisation. If multiple suppliers are coming together into a consortium, it can take time for them to find an effective way to work together. This is analogous to the situation described earlier where the project and business teams need to be welded together into a single team. Here, even within the project team, there are multiple viewpoints, experiences and assumptions that all need to be addressed so that a unified delivery consortium can be effective. Each member may also have had to handle the challenges of a sales handover of variable quality from their respective sales teams, which means that they may not all be starting from the same level of understanding. The fact that a consortium is likely to have a lead organisation and then a potentially complex web of suppliers and supply chain partners injects an additional commercial tension into the project team, which can make 'ego-less' partnering more difficult. All of this bringing together of a consortium to form a project team takes time, especially since they will almost inevitably be geographically separated. International consortia pose even greater co-ordination challenges. The business may not appreciate (or care) about this and will not always have allowed time to do this; nonetheless, such a view from the business does not mean that this activity can be skipped. As such, the project needs to work with the business and educate it about the realities of what will be involved before a large consortium is really in a position to deliver to the business.

A further complex scenario arises when the business client is, in practice, a collection, federation or combination of a number of separate organisations. This can quite often happen with clients in the public sector, where one central body procures a project to be delivered to a number of local organisations, maybe one in each geographical region in a country. Sometimes these local organisations are divisions of the main central organisation, in which case the central body has some authority over them, particularly in terms of achieving agreement to requirements. But in other more complex cases, these local bodies can have considerable autonomy. Where this happens, the central client may have to use powers of advocacy, persuasion or manufactured peer pressure (e.g. publishing a league table of relative performance comparing the local organisations against each other) to reach a situation where all of the local bodies actually agree to what the project is going to deliver. The extent of focus that is then required on stakeholder management can grow quite substantially. There will also be a need to establish ground rules about who does the stakeholder management across the federated client. In some cases the business may delegate this to the project team because it views it as an inconvenient chore, while in other situations the relationship between the central client and the local organisations is highly political and sensitive, so that the central client will not want the project team stepping on its toes and messing up the internal politics. This may suit the central client, but the time needed to work through the internal bargaining on the client side may prove excessive from a project perspective and may slow the rate of progress against what was initially planned and hoped for. In all such situations, the risk of incorrect assumptions again comes into play, as both the project and the business may have assumed one approach to stakeholder management when in fact the other approach was assumed by the other party and either not enough stakeholder management happens or alternatively overkill arises and the stakeholders are bombarded with inconsistent messages from all sides in an unscheduled fashion. Thus, to bridge this potential gap, the core management of the business and the project need to discuss this possibility early and in detail so that sensible agreements can be reached on how this will be approached.

The final and most complex scenario arises when both the delivering project team is formed from a consortium and also the business client is a combination of a number of separate organisations. All of the foregoing considerations above apply, but due to the additional complexity introduced by having consortiums on both sides, additional time will need to be included for establishing agreements, operating effective lines of communication and running decision making mechanisms that balance consulting all of the parties with still making timely forward progress.

One extra complication is that nothing stands still for long. In particular with large teams from potentially a number of organisations, it is quite likely that sooner rather than later there will be a change in one or more of the key personnel. Whenever this happens, some of the activities undertaken to establish the teams and their effective working patterns will need to be repeated. In particular, it is important to re-establish face-to-face working relationships and not to assume that previous ones will automatically carry over and carry on.

WIDER CONTEXT

The project will operate in a context and support environment that can either enhance and empower it or distract and detract from its ability to deliver. This support environment can be provided by the business itself, particularly if the project team and the business are part of the same organisation. Alternatively, if the project team is coming from an external provider, then it will need to support the project team with a certain amount of 'housekeeping' in terms of staff induction, equipment, time tracking and financial systems. Even in this latter situation, it is quite common for a supplier's project team to be based at the client business's premises, which means that the client business will also be involved in making sure that the project team has everything it needs – desks, access to computer systems, the ability to record time and expenses if appropriate, and the ability to schedule meetings and arrange transport. Although apparently run-of-the-mill and administrative in nature, if these areas are not addressed adequately, the project team will find itself frustrated and will not able to get started effectively.

GOVERNANCE

Well-aligned top-level governance structures for an organisation can assist or hinder a project. This applies to the organisation that is providing the project team, but even more so to the business. If there are boards and senior directors (e.g. Chief Operating Officers or Vice Presidents) with responsibility for programme and project management, then an organisation is much more likely to be successful in supporting the project. Where there is a structure that is more traditional and silo-based and does not include any provision for projects, it will inevitably be less well aware, aligned and supportive at a top level of projects in general and the individual project in particular. This can only be a bad thing and will not help the project get established, be well understood or its challenges and achievements fully appreciated.

Key Points

- To the business, the activities involved in getting a project started can seem like excessive slow bureaucracy.

- The role of the business within a project may not be evident to members of the business.

- The business already exists in terms of its structure, organisation and support functions, which is different from a project that usually has to set itself up from scratch.

- When it is starting up, a project has two strands of activity: the early deliverables of the project – mandates, requirements and plans – together with the work involved in setting itself up with staff, facilities and its own working practices.

- If not already settled, the project will need to obtain clear answers to a number of questions:

  - what are we delivering?
  - what is the scope?
  - are the estimates realistic?
  - how are we going to deliver the project?
  - how much time is available?
  - is this buildable?
  - who is going to do what?
  - what environment, tools and infrastructure does the project need?
  - how can we get hold of the people and equipment we need to do the job?

- To bridge the divide, both parties need to understand the points made above and then:

  - understand the importance of attending to small details at the start;
  - establish combined joint teams, fusing the business personnel and the project staff into one team so that they become united and concentrate on tackling shared external challenges;
  - appreciate that as new people join both the business and project part of the teams, that the team's effectiveness will dip and that repeated cycles of effort will be needed to re-establish a cohesive team that can perform effectively;
  - handle the impact on the business of using members of the business on the project – both in terms of disruption to the regular flow of the business and also the extra stress on the business staff who are working in an unfamiliar project style and may still have the old day job making demands upon them;
  - introduce members of the business team to the way that the project works;
  - introduce members of the project team to the way that the business works;
  - projects run to a pattern of activities that is separate from the main business. The phased nature of project activities can feel alien to

someone who is used to a regular routine of work pattern. What matters is to get business members of the team introduced to this and involved from the start;

– invest time and effort in getting agreements, especially contracts, settled as soon as possible;

– make deliberate efforts to build effective teams, taking into account the effects of geographical separation;

– be aware that complex supply chains and members of a consortium can take time to gel together into a single team;

– be cognisant of previous bad experiences that the parties may have had working together and take steps to 'over-write' these by holding combined activities to break down barriers and establish a bond of renewed trust;

– identify stakeholders and work together to actively manage them;

– recheck and reconfirm the alignment of the project timeline and the business's regular cycles;

– establish a strong support environment for the project team – in terms of technology and business functions such as HR, technology, procurement, legal and facilities management;

– make sure top-level governance structures are optimised to help rather than hinder the effective conduct of the project;

– have plans in place to repeat some of these activities whenever new people take up key roles in the business or project.

Chapter 5
Requirements

The Business Perspective

The area of requirements is often one where expectations diverge between the business and the project. Let us start with how the business is likely to view requirements. Remembering that the business is itself not a unified and consistent entity, but rather something that is staffed by a number of individuals with a range of perspectives, it is quite likely that a selection of the views discussed below will be applicable.

IT'S OBVIOUS – I SHOULDN'T NEED TO EXPLAIN THIS TO YOU

This sits at the crux of the requirements conundrum. What is self-evident to someone in the business will not necessarily occur to someone on the project team. This is to do with the extent to which the project team members, particularly those involved in requirements but also in project management, fully appreciate the way in which the business works. The members of the business team who are involved in specifying the requirements are often selected for their deep expert knowledge of the business. They are best placed to appreciate the full ramifications of the choices and trade-offs that are often part of the process of developing requirements. The challenge that relates to this, however, is that such individuals have the business so deeply engrained in their psyche that they hold a lot of their understanding of the business as tacit knowledge. This means that although they understand the business best, they are not necessarily they most effective at articulating how the business currently functions and how it needs to do things differently once the project has delivered.

SHOW ME WHAT'S POSSIBLE

Part of the benefit that comes from undertaking a project is to maximise the art of the possible. If the business is looking to change the way it does things, do new things or create something new, then a project provides the right mechanism to use. People in the business may be so caught up with their current activities that their current way of working inadvertently constrains their thinking about what can be achieved. This can lead to a requirement being described using the 'terminology of today' rather than in a more abstract way in terms of what is to be achieved. It takes insight and self-awareness on the part of the business, but in some situations the business will appreciate that there is merit in an approach to requirements formulation that starts with the request 'show me what is possible'. By doing this the project team can take the business through a number of scenarios for how the changes that are wanted can be achieved. Starting with a very high-level 'helicopter view' of the situation, this approach can yield valuable insights into a range of alternative ways of achieving the desired goal. It levels the playing field by bringing the business up to speed with what is achievable and then enables it to formulate its requirements using the concepts of today and tomorrow rather than being stuck attempting to tinker with the old ways of working.

I'LL KNOW WHAT I WANT WHEN I SEE IT

Closely related to the previous concept, a viewpoint of 'I'll know what I want when I see it' extends the technique of 'show me what is possible'. It reflects the difficulty that people have with visualising and fully appreciating how something new will function if the only description of it is on a static piece of paper. A dynamic real-world example, some sort of prototype, mock-up, model, simulated dry-run or similar approach enables a dry text-based description of a requirement to be turned into something that is much more alive and comprehensible. The challenge here is that until the business sees something in action, it is actually quite hard to know if that is what is really wanted. Often more than one example can help. A single example, when compared to the existing way of doing something, makes it difficult to evaluate and determine if the new approach is the right one. This is where coming up with a range of examples – we can achieve your goal by doing this, doing that or doing the other – provides a situation that can be much more helpful to the business. The contrasting ways of achieving the same goal not only enable the pros and cons to be assessed and compared, but also act as a stimulus to thinking about the original requirement. There is a generally held view that the simplest solution to a problem is often the best, and by generating a range of possible solutions, it will become more obvious which ones are best suited to achieving a simple and effective outcome. The dialogue process that surrounds the development and evaluation of these competing ways of describing the goal is also helpful, as a discussion centred on the concrete examples can provide an effective mechanism to support the convergence of disparate business views around an agreed and shared approach. This is often more effective than attempting to do this by a group of individuals separately reviewing and commenting on a dry document that runs the risk of misunderstanding and not achieving a shared viewpoint.

IT'S HARD TO EXPLAIN

'It's hard to explain' can be quite frustrating for a project team, but nonetheless it is also not good for the business. This is a combination of some of the earlier considerations whereby a lot of the knowledge about how things are currently done and how they need to be done in the future is tacit and potentially spread across a collection of people within the business. This is where the project can assist by introducing language and techniques that can help to illuminate, unpack and clarify what the requirements really are. Sometimes requirements are hard to explain because they relate to deeply specialised and highly complex problem domains, such as advanced science or financial trading, which need sophisticated mathematics to enable the problem to be specified, modelled and resolved. In other cases the project may be changing a situation that has previously been in existence for a very long time and, as a result, it hardly documented at all. Everyone knows what they do – whenever a problem arises, there is someone who has seen it before and knows how to tackle it. The business is a well-oiled machine and in effect is self-managing and prospers without the need for a detailed rulebook or set of instructions. When faced with this sort of situation, the project has to invest effort in fully understanding the current 'as-is' arrangements. This enables the requirements to be built on firm foundations. There is then less likelihood that one of the new requirements will inadvertently change the way of working in such a fashion as to severely disrupt the business's core operations. There is a balance to be struck here, as it may appear to the business that the project is focusing on the present at the expense of the future. The project team needs to explain to the business the risks that are associated with skimping on this activity of understanding of current world. All of these considerations together enable the challenge of 'it's hard to explain' to be reduced to something manageable.

I'M NOT SURE WHO KNOWS

The scenario of 'I'm not sure who knows' may not always arise, but does so more often than one might expect. It parallels the situation of 'I'll know when I see it' in the sense that there is a recognition by the business that the person or team leading the creation of the requirements is not necessarily in possession of all the information that is needed. The challenge here is that it may not be clear who does know the answer to a particular aspect. The process for tracking down such a person, presuming for the moment that they do exist, is not always easy to predict and factor into the timeline of the project. This can mean that the business, as it goes about creating the requirements, can introduce delays to this stage of the project, which might not have been included in the initial planning estimates. This can be an area in which the members of the project team can feel frustrated because they may not be able to help the business in tracking down who has the requirement information. Certainly their knowledge of the business will be poorer than the business team. What the project team may be able to assist with is simply the provision of people, who, rather than distracting members of the business from their day jobs, can invest the time and effort needed to work their way across the organisation to locate the individuals who are in a position to clarify the currently unknown points. In the worst-case scenario, where no answer can be found, it is better to know this early in the project lifecycle so that the situation can be taken into account in terms of assumptions and planning. A determination may need to be made as to whether not knowing this particular piece of information is in any way a 'showstopper' and what work-arounds may be needed in order to enable to project to still be undertaken.

IT'S NOT YET CERTAIN, CAN WE JUST GET STARTED?

Faced with a situation where 'It's not yet certain, can we just get started?', the project has some tricky choices to make. This is often inherent in the lifecycle of a project, particularly for a project that is making changes to an organisation and the way in which it will function and undertake particular activities in the future. There may not be the time available to work out everything in advance. There may be external factors which are running to their own timeline and will not be known until sometime after the project has got going. This means that the requirements will need to be analysed and categorised according to certainty, and where they are not fully certain, a forecast date should be sought for when such certainty is expected to be achieved. This will not be a perfect forecast, but having it is better than not having it. This situation may alter the shape of the project in terms of what is to be created in what sequence. Quite often projects have a natural best sequence of tasks, in terms of what is done in what order, and an analysis of the full requirements enables this to almost fall out as a byproduct. However, if some requirements are not going to be known fully until a later date and there is no way of taking additional action to bring this date nearer, then the sequence of the project activities will need to be adjusted. It may end up being sub-optimal, but this compromise will at least enable the project to get started and make forward progress on the areas that are known. Care will need to be taken not to 'paint the project into a corner' in respect of what is not yet known. Finding the balance point may need quite active and senior discussion about the risks associated with getting started in areas where there is uncertainty. There is no right or wrong answer here – the key point is that the risks of no action versus the risks of taking action that might need to be undone once certainty is available need to be discussed, weighed and assessed. Provided that this is done with the full informed participation of the project and business senior management teams, everyone will have contributed to a shared view on what is the most appropriate way forwards and the project will have made the best accommodation that it can to the situation where not everything is known fully from day one.

THERE IS TOO MUCH TO TAKE IN ALL IN ONE GO

'There is too much to take in all in one go' is a perfectly reasonable reaction from the business. Experienced project staff are used to thinking in a particular way about a situation. They tend to operate in multiple parallel dimensions at the same time:

- a requirements perspective – modelling the whole of the 'as-is' and also the 'to-be' situation;

- a timeline perspective – juggling the many project tasks into a sequence that makes sense;

- a financial perspective – assessing the payment the project will receive and the costs it will incur;

- together with further viewpoints in some situations.

For individuals from the business who have not been exposed to this way of working before, the whole thing can feel like being thrown into the swimming pool at the deep end. Often requirements can be captured in a document that can run to many chapters, sections and tens or hundreds of pages. Project staff who are used to such documents may overlook the fact that to the uninitiated, such hefty tomes can be quite daunting. Indeed, for everyone, both business and project, garnering a full understanding and an appreciation of them can be difficult. This is where the ability to split requirements into layers of abstraction, and group particular requirements together where they have certain aspects in common, can create a more digestible set of requirements. The additional use of alternate ways to characterise a requirement – models, prototypes and dry-runs of new processes in a workshop – can all make a large set of dry documentation more comprehensible.

WHY DO WE NEED THIS MUCH DETAIL?

'Why do we need this much detail?' can come as a complaint from the business. This is a symptom of the project not having taken the business with it on the journey to explain how the project needs to be run for it to be successful. As with earlier considerations, running a pre-existing organisation, with a well-established set of processes, is perfectly possible with a combination of individual expertise, tacit knowledge and common sense. The creation of a new way of working often takes the existing processes and, in order to create new versions of them, unpacks and analyses the 'as-is' and 'to-be' situation in greater detail than is required for day-to-day operations.

THIS IS GIVING TOO MUCH FOCUS TO WHAT CAN GO WRONG

The need for detail and analysing the requirements thoroughly can provoke an unexpected response from the business along the lines of 'this is giving too much focus to what can go wrong, I want to concentrate on how this will work properly'. The detailed analysis is needed to make sure that all the consequences of the proposed changes that are part of the requirements have been identified and understood, and that nothing negative or unexpected is going to arise. It is also a feature of any project that is seeking to increase the level of automation of a process, particularly by the use of IT. In such circumstances the main flow through the process is the one that the business concentrates upon. There will be problems and exceptions, but experienced human intervention can resolve these; however, for an automated system, each problem situation will need to be pre-defined and a response designed and created. This is where, in the eyes of the business, the level of detail and analysis can appear excessive. It can also seem negative as it is focusing upon all the different ways in which a process can go wrong. Although necessary in order to make sure that everything in the new world will run smoothly, this nonetheless feels like a 'glass half empty' way of looking at things. A business motivated by a strong positive culture, focused upon performance and success, may find such an approach – identifying the minutiae of failure – as counter to its spirit. This is where dialogue between the project and the business again becomes important, as each needs a greater appreciation of the other's perspective on their way of seeing the future delivered by the project.

WHY DO I NEED TO READ THIS MASSIVE REQUIREMENTS DOCUMENT?

The final area of business frustration can often surface when the results of the requirements analysis work are assembled together into a document (often a requirements specification), which, as mentioned above, can become quite lengthy. As a result, the business may react by saying: 'Why do I need to read this massive requirements document? I'm busy enough already with my day job'. Such a situation needs to be prevented if at all possible, as turning the requirements into a hurdle is not helpful for either party. Careful structuring can often help here, with summary introductions and then particular sections targetted at specific parts of the business. This means that most members of the business team will not need to read, digest and agree to the whole requirements document, but rather only the sections that relate to their areas of concern and expertise. In most cases very few members of the business team will have the time to read such a document (their day job will simply be too demanding), so the project needs to plan on this basis and incorporate other methods of conveying the requirements to the business so as to confirm that they are correct. The project plan tends to be created by the members of the project team, who assign reasonable amounts to time to their tasks, but can overlook the equivalent effort required by the business and only give a token day or so of effort to the business for approval tasks. So, in addition, the project should not assume that the business will be able to quickly and simply agree to the requirements document; thus, the project timelines in the planned schedules should take this into account and include time for understanding, discussion, amendment, revision and convergence on final agreement.

The Project Perspective

Having considered the business perspective, we now turn our attention to the other half of the partnership. A project is a time-bound and resource-constrained set of activities with a very specific focus of providing an agreed outcome via a set of deliverables. To achieve this demanding goal, it is absolutely essential that a project is able to get its requirements fully sorted out. From a project perspective, what then constitutes a good set of requirements? They need to satisfy a number of criteria:

- Complete.

- Unambiguous.

- Able to be validated.

- Prioritised.

- Traceable.

- Adjustable.

- Clarifiable.

- Current.

Let us examine each of these in turn.

COMPLETE

The requirements need to cover the whole of the 'problem space' that the project is addressing. This can have a number of dimensions in terms of what is to be delivered by the project to the business:

- Physical items – a building, machinery, land.

- Processes – new ways of working, which would include process descriptions and training material.

- People – either newly added to the organisation, trained in new processes, with increased levels of motivation or made redundant from the organisation.

- Near-physical items – software and computer-related items.

- Services – in their many forms.

- Abstract items – such as changes in legal ownership and simply information.

- Inevitably, documentation relating to all of the above.

There may be other categories of required deliverables – these are simply illustrative of the range of items that the project has to take into consideration. Once the analysis of the requirements gets underway, it starts to become clear that it is not nearly as obvious as it might seem, and the ability to declare that a complete set of requirements has been created is actually quite a challenge.

A related aspect is sometimes known as functional versus non-functional requirements. There is often a focus on the functional requirements, which cover what the solution that the project is delivering will do. If it is a process, this would be the process steps; if it were a new organisation, then it would be the new organisation chart and the employees correctly employed in their new roles. Non-functional requirements are sometimes overlooked and, to the unfamiliar eye, can appear to be rather pedantic and detailed. Nonetheless, they are needed for a complete set of requirements. They relate to features of a solution covering a range of aspects, such as the following:

- Availability – when is the service to operate? All the time or only during office hours Monday to Friday?

- Capacity – how many clients can be served at the same time?

- Business continuity – if a disaster happens at the location where the solution is based, how long can it not be running for? If only part of it can be restarted quickly, then which part?

- Scalability – if the business being supported by the solution grows, how easy must it be for the solution to grow with it?

There are many types of non-functional requirement, and the list above is highly selective and included for illustration purposes only. The key point is that the requirements are not complete unless all of the relevant non-functional aspects have been considered.

UNAMBIGUOUS

There are many spheres of business and political life where ambiguity can be useful, helping to smooth a disagreement or move a situation forward. For a project that wants to provide a set of deliverables within an agreed timeframe and budget, ambiguity is not helpful.

Areas of ambiguity can include the boundaries of the project. This relates to what it is going to deliver and what the business or other third parties are going to provide. This is where requirements need to have sections dedicated to scope. It is quite common for there to be lists of what is in scope and also what is out of scope. This helps to minimise confusion and doubt amongst all the participating parties. Items can cross the scope boundary as part of the requirements development process, as reviewers of draft requirements discover that items are in or out of scope incorrectly and their status is redefined in newer drafts ahead of agreeing the final requirements. This can have significant ramifications for a project if an assumption has been made about a set of items being out of scope, with budgets and timelines developed on this basis, and then they move in scope, knocking the whole project into a different shape and calendar.

A further consideration is the fact that for any non-trivial solution, a project will end up with a large number of requirements. Each may make sense on its own, but soon, as their number grows, it will be difficult for one person to keep all of them in mind and to be able to form a unified view about them. Quite often, different sets of requirements are developed by different people, sometimes spread across both the business and the project. The result of all of this is that when taken as a whole, the requirements set may start to develop internal inconsistencies. At a simple level, some may be easy to spot – for instance, the requirement to be available every day of the year, but also a need to have a day of downtime once every three months. Others may be much harder if there are large amounts of complex logic spread around a systems solution, and will a require knowledgeable team review of the complete set of requirements – often in a workshop setting – to uncover. Once identified, these diverging requirements can be reconciled, but it is important that such clashes are spotted at this time, as fixing them later when a solution has been designed and built will be much more complicated, time-consuming and expensive.

The other aspect of ambiguity avoidance is clarity. Where requirements are written in narrative text, they are sometimes not easy to understand. In other cases, although they make initial sense, it can turn out that there are multiple interpretations possible from them, and different readers are able to assume differing final outcomes as a result. To avoid this, projects tend to move away from just using narrative text and adopt more formal methods of describing what is required. These can include many different sorts of diagrams, flowcharts, maps and drawings. A different type of presentation is more tabular in nature and combines built-in logic to make sure that if there are a number of routes through a process, all the possible combinations of inputs and choices have been considered and an outcome specified for each situation. This level of precision comes at a price, because such analysis techniques – although reducing the risk of ambiguity – make it much harder for the lay reader to follow, understand and agree to the requirements. The project needs to make a decision about whether, having undertaken this level of requirements analysis, it will present it to the business for agreement and, if it does so, whether first it will need to invest in some training for representatives from the business in the techniques used so that they are in a comfortable position and are able to make an informed judgement about the requirements without getting lost in the analysis method.

ABLE TO BE VALIDATED

There are various ways to express a set of requirements. From a project perspective, they will not be fit for purpose unless they can be validated. This means that they must be expressed (usually written) in such a way that they can be clearly demonstrated as being met. These checks often take the form of tests, and for the tests to be effective, the requirements that lead to the creation of the test need to support the clear specification of a set of tests. It needs to be obvious to an independent observer, based upon reproducible evidence, whether a requirement has been met or not, and this is usually done by undertaking a number of observations and/or tests. If the requirements are not able to be validated, there will be scope for disagreement within the business and between the business and the project as to whether the project has delivered what was required of it.

PRIORITISED

When a set of requirements are put together, a long list often develops. Some requirements are at the very core of what the project is delivering, and without them being met, nothing would actually be achieved. Others are more at the periphery of the solution – it could operate without them, but it might be better with them. Quite often projects develop lists of requirements, sometimes referred to as catalogues, held in tabular format or some sort of database. These enable some features or attributes of the requirements to be captured and retained along with the actual requirement. This is where the prioritisation element is often recorded, with a label such as Mandatory, Preferred or Optional. In other situations a requirements level of priority can be identified using the words with which it is expressed, which can include must, should or could.

There is a closely related dimension to priority, which is sequencing. This arises where a project splits its deliveries into more than one phase, sometimes referred to as a 'drop'. In this situation all the requirements are probably mandatory, but they are not all delivered at the same time. There can be subtleties to this where the first phase delivers all the mandatory requirements and, if there is sufficient time and budget left, subsequent phases then move on to delivering the preferred and then the optional requirements.

The important point is that thinking about this is done at the requirements assembly phase of the project so that both the project and the business know that what they are focusing upon are the most important aspects and that they are sequenced correctly.

TRACEABLE

The journey from requirement to deliverable is rarely simply and straightforward. There are usually quite a number of intermediate steps:

- often involving a requirement – which tends to be expressed as an outcome (i.e. what something will do);

- being turned into a design (i.e. how the what will be done);

- which in turn is translated into an individual element of the solution (something that is built or created or changed);

- which is then checked or tested to confirm that it aligns with the design;

- which is then assembled together with other elements to provide the solution;

- which, as a whole, needs to be checked back against the original requirement.

This journey from requirement to solution is spread out over time (sometimes quite an extended period of time) and the individual tasks within it may be undertaken by different individuals, each with skills appropriate to that step in the journey. As a result, the path taken by the requirement through the project lifecycle can become obscured.

To avoid this, an element of traceability can be added. This involves uniquely labelling each distinct requirement with some sort of identifier, often a number or combination of numbers and letters, developed centrally within the project, so that all the requirements have unique identifiers. These can then be used to trace the requirement through the lifecycle. Similar approaches are then taken to the design elements, to the actual build deliverables and to the validation and testing activities. Analyses can then be undertaken to identify which design elements expand upon a given requirement, which build elements correspond to a design, and which validation activities and tests check that a given requirement has been met. The relationships are often not one-to-one – a given requirement may require many design elements, some of which may also at the same time meet other requirements. The same many-to-many pattern can continue so that a build element can achieve the requirements for more than one design element and so on.

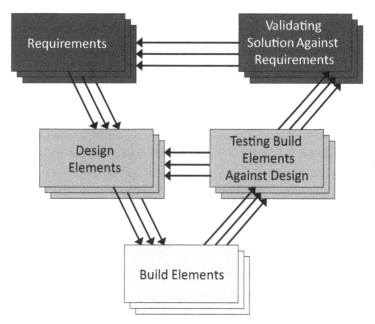

Figure 5.1   Tracing between requirements, design, build, test and validation

The result of this, although appearing to be complicated, actually helps to cut a path through the inherent complexity of the project enabling the relationship between the requirement and the outcome to be traced and tracked with certainty throughout the lifecycle of the project.

ADJUSTABLE

Projects are rarely so short that the full set of original requirements remains complete and valid at the end. Something will have changed either in the external world or in the evolving knowledge of the project that leads to certain requirements needing to be adjusted. The way in which requirements are structured and expressed can assist or frustrate such adjustments. If a system is being developed, it could be stated that it will need to be available for 500 users. If during the project there is an organisational change and the system now needs to be available to 1,000 users, this may present significant problems. To avoid such a situation, the requirement could be expressed in such a way as to say that the system must support at least 500 users and be capable of expansion easily without making major changes so that the number of users can be increased to up to 2,000 without needing to re-engineer the system. The underlying objective is for requirements to be gathered and expressed in a way that does not paint the project into a corner, but rather gives it flexibility to respond to evolving circumstances in the future.

CLARIFIABLE

Some requirements may be rather uncertain to start with. Where this is the case and the earlier approaches to obtaining a fully known unambiguous requirement prove difficult, one additional aspect needs to be considered. This relates to expressing it in a way so that it can be clarified in the future as the project progresses. Sometimes the natural progress of the project and the increasing level of knowledge lead to a requirement that is clearer. In other cases deliberate action is needed – this can consist of some combination of experimentation, piloting, iteration and testing. Experimentation will try out special cases of the requirement to see if a better version of it can be derived. Piloting may involve actually making a choice between alternatives within the requirement and trying one of these out in within the business. Iteration recognises that some projects are best delivered in a series of waves or iterations; in this case parts of the requirement are addressed, designed, built, tested and implemented; based on the experience of this, then next part of the requirement is then addressed. Testing involves actively dry-running a requirement in a simulation (either on paper, in a workshop of people or on a computer) to determine whether it is appropriate and thus to clarify it. The technique used to clarify the requirement is less important than the recognition that some requirements start out as obscure and vague and need to be expressed in a way that means they can be actively refined until clear.

CURRENT

As has been said before, all projects take time – some more than others. The steps from identifying a project, getting it started and then assembling a complete set of requirements can easily range over weeks, if not a few months. The initial set of requirements may well have been up-to-date when the project was first considered, but it is quite possible that events will overtake some of them quite quickly. It is therefore key to make sure that as part of the requirements approval process, which results in a set of frozen requirements that can be used as a firm starting point for the design, that the requirements are fully up-to-date.

The project will then move into its subsequent phases, involving design, build, test and implementation. This will also take time. During this period the context around the project and the knowledge within it will evolve and change. The requirements-set that was previously agreed and frozen may need to be changed. This is not a sign of failure, but a recognition that the solution needs to reflect the real world and be adjusted if the world moves on. This does, however, necessitate a key project discipline known as change control in which any adjustments to any document (or set of documents) that is agreed and frozen, sometimes known as a baseline, is done according to a formal process which identifies what is to be changed, what the impacts of this change will be in terms of scope, finances and timescales, and gains the formal approval of all parties to this before creating a new updated version of the controlled document which is also then frozen and becomes the new baseline.

CONCLUSION

Having examined the attributes that the project concerns itself with when the requirements are put together, there is one other consideration that the project can face. It may be challenged with a set of requirements that ask for something to be created or built or delivered that is unproven. There may be no evidence or track record that something the same has been done before. This introduces a degree of uncertainty because the project may not know if it can create the required deliverables. In this case the requirements will need to reflect this degree of challenge and take account of the fact that the chances of the project succeeding are not as predictable as they would be where the project is repeating a template of change that has already been successfully implemented elsewhere.

Bridging the Divide

Having examined the business and the project views of requirements, which can be quite divergent and tend to have different agendas, we now need to address how to bridge the divide. There are a range of techniques that are worth including – some obvious, some less so. The essence of the approach will be pragmatism aimed at building a joint viewpoint of the requirements that enables the project to move forward together based on a firm foundation. The following techniques merit discussion:

- Talking.

- Testing of assumptions.

- Demonstrations.

- Iteration.

- Segmenting.

- Freezing.

- Agreements.

- Achievement.

- Avoiding tripwires.

- Using accelerators.

TALKING

This may seem obvious, but talking is the foundation of any successful approach to bridging the divide. There is a tendency for projects, particularly large ones or geographically separated ones, to rely too heavily on documents and email. The essence of the requirements creation process is the joint assembly of a set of agreed requirements that the project is able to implement to the agreed quality, timescale and budget. As they are identified, they are inevitably captured in one or more documents. When a project and the business are separated by anything more than being on different floors of the same building, the temptation to use email to circulate the requirements becomes overwhelming. This can often interact with a document review process, involving forms and written comments against the document, that is useful in that it gives formal traceability to all comments, but is also one that can lead to position-taking, the raising of many questions and the evolution of a game of 'document tennis'.

Document tennis happens where a set of comments is raised and the document is updated to reflect those comments, but the reviewers are either unhappy with the amendments or also identify further points that they want clarified, changed or addressed. The cycle can continue for quite a few iterations. Often more and more people get dragged into the review process because it is easy to copy in someone on email or for a reviewer to forward a document on to an additional person. The weakness of this process is that it can become quite confrontational, with the document being bounced back and forth between the business and the project rather like a ball being hit back and forth across a tennis court.

The additional element that is required here is talking. There are now a wide variety of methods, but the most preferable is still face-to-face, as it enables the full range of communication styles to be used without the loss of non-verbal cues. The nature and variety of elements within non-verbal communications are explored in considerable detail in Mehrabian (2007); it is sufficient for our purposes to observe that the available channels diminish as physical separation is introduced, and diminish further when video and audio mechanisms are removed, leaving simply the written word. If a number of inputs are required, a facilitated workshop-style meeting can be very effective. This type of meeting can bring to the surface shared concerns, expose comments to scrutiny, weigh different requirements against each other, test the validity of assumptions and in the end reach a reconciled, self-consistent and balanced set of requirements. The use of a facilitator in such an environment is helpful as they can take a neutral stance, balance the views of the project and the business, and have no political axe to grind apart from ensuring that the requirements are agreed – amicably wherever possible – within the allotted timeframe.

TESTING OF ASSUMPTIONS

The testing of assumptions merits separate attention. Both the business and the project will have made assumptions about the requirements. These may be explicit and documented in some sort of Assumptions Register, or they may be implicit, held tacitly within the requirements documentation but not articulated clearly. However, just gathering and recording assumptions is insufficient.

Each party needs to be clear about its own assumptions, but in particular to bridge the divide, it needs to fully understand the other party's assumptions. This may form part of the same workshop as mentioned above in 'Talking' or it may need to be separate. What is essential is that the project first of all understands the assumptions that the business has made, then considers their implications for the project and either accepts them or challenges the business on them so that the assumption can be explored in greater depth and agreement reached on how to handle it. The reverse process then needs to happen, with the business considering and where it feels it necessary to challenge the project's assumptions. One notable result of this can be that it transpires that each party has made an assumption that contradicts that of the other party. At the simplest level, this could be that the business assumed that the project was going to do a particular task, whilst the project assumed that the business was going to do this. Without testing the assumptions, this could easily have fallen down the gap in the middle and not been done by either party, with the omission of the task being discovered too late and its remediation taking more time and money than it would otherwise have needed.

DEMONSTRATIONS

To achieve a shared understanding of what a set of requirements represents, the value of bringing the solution to life cannot be under-estimated. The way in which this is done will, by necessity, vary with the nature of the solution that the project is providing. A computer system may be capable of being developed in a very cut-down version, possibly with fake screenshots, which can be used to explore walkthroughs of the system during requirements meetings. A new organisation structure can be created using project and business team members role-playing new positions in the organisation and considering how the people in these roles might handle a range of scenarios. A new process can be dry-run using a similar role-play approach. A new product, building or engineering item can be modelled using an appropriate virtual reality tool in order to show how it would function in real life. The level of detail that these demonstrations go down into will vary, but what is significant is that, in doing them, the business and the project will have something concrete around which to base conversations and assessments of the solution. This is greatly preferable to the situation in which all of the analysis and decisions that relate to the requirements are done using only documentation to capture and describe the solution.

ITERATION

There are occasions when projects are either too big to comprehend all in one go or are too big to build. There may be a mismatch between what the members of the project team, who have experience in this sort of thing, think can be achieved and what the business would like. This mismatch can go either way, in that the project may be comfortable with building something significant, but the business less so, or alternatively the business may want a large one-stop solution to all its problems, but the project team, having had experience of problems with delivering similar large undertakings before, may have misgivings.

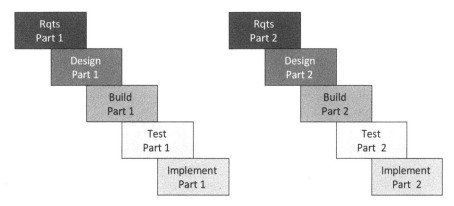

Part 1 completely implemented before work starts on Part 2

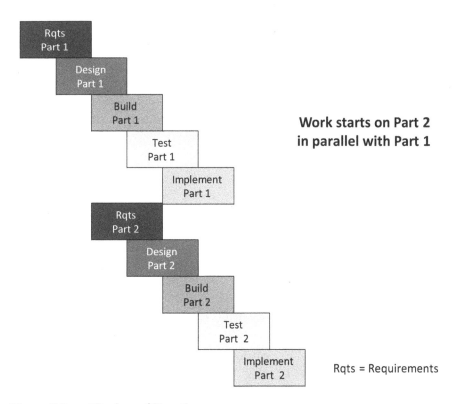

**Work starts on Part 2
in parallel with Part 1**

Rqts = Requirements

Figure 5.2   Timing of iterations

In either situation, one way to reach an effective compromise is to settle on an approach of iteration. This involves partitioning the problem and the requirements into a number of related smaller problems and thus requirement sets. These smaller constituent problems can be sequenced into a priority order. The first of these can then be worked on with its requirements being developed, followed by the design, build, test and implement phases leading to a working solution to the first segment of the requirements. The next set of requirements is then assessed and the process repeated. It may be shortened in duration as the first solution may form either part or all of the start point for building the solution to address the second set of requirements. This process then iterates through as many sets of requirements as were identified in the initial partitioning activity. The timing of the iteration can vary: in some cases all effort is devoted to the first solution until it is fully implemented, and then the second solution is started; in other cases once the first solution is underway as a project, the requirements assessment work for the second solution is then started.

The result of all of this is that the large set of requirements that relate to the project is divided down into manageable chunks, which both the business and the project can understand comfortably, and which are more likely to be implemented successfully. In addition, because they are more understandable, agreement is more likely to be achievable between the business and the project. There is also a beneficial byproduct whereby the lessons that are learnt from the sub-project that addresses the first set of requirements can be fed into the second project, and so on down the chain, so that the later sub-projects can benefit substantially from the lessons learnt by the earlier projects.

SEGMENTING

Segmenting is closely related to but slightly different from iteration. It is an approach that looks to gather, analyse and agree all the requirements upfront, but then split the design, build, test and implementation into separate projects.

This scenario tends to arise when the problem is so interdependent that all aspects of it have to be defined at the same time in order to ensure that they can all work together successfully. That said, some solutions can be built in a phased manner. This may relate to creating all the features of a system, but only making some available initially, following up with later releases that

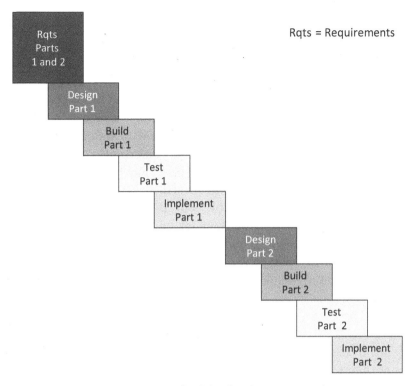

Rqts = Requirements

All requirements identified for both Part 1 and Part 2
Part 1 then completely implemented before work starts on Part 2

Figure 5.3   Segmenting requirements into two projects

turn on more functionality. It might also cover situations in which there are multiple geographies into which the solution is to be delivered; it will be the same solution, but it is easiest if some locations get started first and others follow on later using a structured timetable. For this approach to work, the business needs to buy into this phasing. If this can be achieved, then the result will be a situation in which a controlled roll-out of the solution will give the business a way of phasing in the new solution.

It is worth noting that coming out of the IT field there is an extensive body of knowledge that relates to the approaches of iteration and segmenting, which are collectively referred to as Agile (Beck et al. 2001) project management. Particular techniques that have well-developed literature around them include the Dynamic Systems Development Method (DSDM Atern) (DSDM 2008) and Scrum (Schwaber and Sutherland 2013).

FREEZING

There has already been discussion about agreeing a set of requirements and then freezing or baselining them. To enable good project–business interworking, an adult approach needs to be taken to realise that in many projects it will not always be possible to agree everything. In such situations it may be necessary to freeze certain aspects of the project and in effect to 'agree to disagree' (or more optimistically 'agree to not yet agree'). This can also apply to areas of uncertainty which are not critical but which also cannot be resolved within the timeframe needed to get the requirements settled. In such cases, the project and business together need to acknowledge this situation and work out a joint mechanism for agreeing what remains uncertain, how this uncertainty can be resolved, when this resolution is (a) possible and (b) needed by, and understanding and accepting the consequences of continuing on with the project if the uncertainty cannot be resolved.

AGREEMENTS

Having just discussed a special case of 'agreeing to disagree', it is well worth expanding this to consider the general process for agreement between the business and the project. At the start of the requirements phase, the business and the project need to confirm a common shared method for reaching agreement on all aspects of the project. This needs to involve making sure that all players are included, aware when something is agreed and can find the agreed version of the relevant item. The mechanism that is put in place needs to have suitably empowered individuals who can arbitrate, over-rule and take an executive decision on requirements and other aspects where needed.

ACHIEVEMENT

The final technique that merits consideration is how the achievement of the requirements is going to be proved. Thinking about this at the start helps keep everyone focused on the end goal, which can be tricky as a complex project will have many intermediate detailed distractions. Documentation that sits alongside the requirements and consists of statements of the form 'if there is evidence of X, then requirement Y is deemed to have been met' can give a very valuable anchor point onto which to hang the rest of the project. If both the project and the business are able to agree this document upfront, when hopefully levels of antagonism are at their lowest (and ideally non-existent), then both the business and the project will be on the same page when it comes to agreeing that the project has delivered what was expected of it.

TRIPWIRES AND ACCELERATORS

There are also a number of tripwires that can catch the people out. Similarly, there are a range of accelerators which if applied can push the project forward. These are listed here to prompt thought, although not all of them will apply to any one project.

Sometimes the size of a project is such that from a business perspective, some elements form a relatively small percentage of the overall budget. However, such elements may be pivotal, such as when an engineering system also includes custom-designed software to control it. The physical building and engineering may cost many times more than the software, but the software needs to operate correctly for the project to deliver successfully. The business may allocate oversight of the software to a more junior member of the business team, given that as a percentage of the budget, it is relatively small. In doing so, this can result in an inexperienced member of the business making crucial decisions about the software that is to control the overall solution. This can lead to risks in terms of the requirements, particularly depending upon their knowledge of change control, as they may be less experienced at getting the business to a point where it can agree on a firm and frozen set of requirements. Thus, it is important to be clear about who controls what in terms of the different types of requirements.

The business can often range in style and culture across different departments and functions. This may not always be evident to the project team, who may assume that the same style of interaction and decision making applies consistently across the business. This can lead to the project treating everyone in the business in the same way, which may actually hamper the discovery of, clarification on and agreement on the final requirements.

If a project needs to redesign a process being performed by the business, one approach to getting started that is sometimes overlooked is to 'walk the floor'. This involves actually following an individual item through the existing process from start to finish, talking with each of the people who handled it and changed it. In doing so, the project team can discuss with each member of the business involved in the process what currently works well and what needs to be improved from their perspective. This can give the requirements analysis activity a solid grounding in what goes on at present so that the project has a thorough understanding of the 'as-is' state before it goes on to specify the requirements for the 'to-be' situation.

One particular type of project with a particular flavour of requirements is a consolidation project. This can result from a merger where a new organisation finds that multiple units are sometimes performing the same activity in different ways, and a single approach will be beneficial in terms of both efficiency and effectiveness. The challenge for the project is how to balance the viewpoints from the different parts of the business so that the requirements embody the best way for the new business to work, without alienating staff coming from parts of the organisation that used to work differently.

Beware that for large complex projects, applying change control to requirements and the associated adjustments to costs can prove to be a nightmare. Sometimes getting to a set of stable requirements can involve going deep into design and then iterating back to requirements. If this is going to be the most suitable approach, then for the project and the business, doing this under fixed-price conditions can be a recipe for antagonism and disaster. It is best in this situation to use time and materials pricing to get to the point of stable requirements, and only then to use a fixed-price approach.

If a project is covering multiple sectors or geographies, the business or the project may be tempted to make assumptions that a 'one-size-fits-all' set of requirements is possible. Quite often a solution that works well in one sector or geographical area will not necessarily translate smoothly and successfully into another. It is better to start with this in mind as then local sensitivities can be taken into account, and the eventual roll-out and adoption are likely to be more successful.

If the business is faced with problems trying to clarify what its real requirements are, then getting two or three vendors of competing solutions to work up demonstrations can help not only to choose between them, but also to explore, clarify and confirm requirements before engaging one and getting started in earnest.

Where there is a complex delivery structure for a project with a number of organisations forming a consortium to compete to undertake a project, it will take time for the project team to really get started. In particular at the early stages of a project, a multi-supplier bid team can take a while to get together, understand the requirements and put forward a coherent solution. This can be exacerbated if the client is not yet fully clear on what they want. The result is that iterations of what is possible and what is required will be needed before a sensible and complete set of requirements, which the consortium is comfortable that it can deliver, will emerge.

Change is inevitable during the time that it takes a project to move from inception to delivery. In particular, the staff on the business side who generated the requirements can leave the project arena, either to do a different role in other parts of the business or simply leaving the business completely. This can lead to requirements that were raised by such individuals becoming 'orphaned' (in a way that is similar to the 'orphan benefits' described by Driver (2014)). The project can find itself in a situation where there is no longer a champion in the business for a particular requirement, possibly even no one who really understands what the aim of the requirement was and how it should be achieved. One way to avoid this is to give every requirement an individual owner in the business during the requirements gathering and analysis process. The project team will then need to periodically check during the evolution of the project if any of the business requirement owners have left the arena. Where this happens, such requirements will need to be given a new business owner, who genuinely wants to own the requirement and can continue to sponsor, understand and explain the requirement to the project. If it is not possible to find a new owner to take on the requirement, then it may be necessary to remove it from the project, using appropriate change control mechanisms.

Business staff sometimes have an instruction dropped on to them to undertake a project without their senior management appreciating that the business staff have not done projects before and will need training and assistance in order to deliver it. This means that when being approached by the business with a requirement to undertake a project, the project team needs to make sure it is clear on how well the business team understands the project, together with how well the project team understands the business. Only with good two-way understanding can the requirements be crafted and agreed and the project move forward into design.

Key Points

- The area of requirements is often one where expectations diverge between the business and the project.

- The business is staffed by a number of individuals with a range of perspectives that are likely to span the following:

  - it's obvious – I shouldn't need to explain this to you;
  - show me what's possible;
  - I'll know what I want when I see it;

- it's hard to explain;
- I'm not sure who knows;
- it's not yet certain, can we just get started?;
- there is too much to take in all at one go;
- why do we need this much detail?
- this is giving too much focus to what can go wrong;
- why do I need to read this massive requirements document?

- From a project perspective, a good set of requirements need to satisfy a number of criteria:

  - complete;
  - unambiguous;
  - able to be validated;
  - prioritised;
  - traceable;
  - adjustable;
  - clarifiable;
  - current.

- To bridge the divide, both parties need to understand the points made above and then use a range of techniques to identify and confirm the requirements:

  - talking;
  - testing of assumptions;
  - demonstrations;
  - iteration;
  - segmenting;
  - freezing;
  - using an agreement process;
  - proof of achievement;
  - avoiding tripwires;
  - using accelerators.

Chapter 6
Design

The Business Perspective

The design phase of a project can be where a shift in emphasis emerges, with the focus of the project moving from the business team across to the project team. It involves translating the requirements, expressed in the language of the business, into a set of detailed descriptions of what needs to be created. These detailed descriptions – the designs – are expressed in the language of the builders; by builders we mean the members of the project team who create the deliverables for the project. They can be hardware engineers, software designers, civil engineers, business process consultants, HR experts or any of a number of other technical disciplines. This change in language is one of the first steps along the journey which can disenfranchise the business.

The use of technical design language is essential if the deliverables are to be created effectively, using the full skill set and expert due diligence of the builders. However, there are a number of consequences to this that affect the business.

TECHNICAL COMPLEXITY

The levels of technical complexity associated with the design stage can make the activity incomprehensible to the business. Various members of the business team will react in different ways to this. Some parts of the business that are particularly focused on the day job will be content to let the project get on with converting the requirements into a buildable design. This part of the organisation will be comfortable with the idea that the project team knows what it is doing and can be safely left to get on with it. This element within the business is more likely to be comfortable with managing by exception and only becoming involved in the design at the instigation of the project team if a problem arises that needs its input.

There may be a second viewpoint within the business that takes a contrary position. This is likely to comprise individuals within the business who also have some technical knowledge relevant to the project, or those with a greater interest in detail, or those with a stronger focus on controlling the project team. All of these players may want to have a deeper involvement in the design. In principle, this may be beneficial to eventual project outcomes, but it very much depends upon the extent to which an effective way of working together during the design phase can be developed.

Misunderstandings and frustration are likely to arise within the business if the project is not clear who within the business falls into each camp:

- People within the business who do not want to know this level of information or detail will get annoyed with the project placing excessive demands upon them if the project does not realise this and over-involves them in the analysis and decision making that will be needed in the design activity.

- People from the business with a strong interest in the design will become increasingly unhappy if they consider that the project is forging ahead without taking the time to involve and consult them in the design activity.

Neither outcome is good for the eventual success of the project or the adoption and successful use of its deliverables by the business.

REQUIREMENTS OVERHANG

As discussed in the preceding chapter, the requirements process can include areas of ambiguity and uncertainty. Sometimes these cannot be clarified fully without starting to undertake some of the design work.

This overhang from the requirements activities can lead to business team members being dragged unexpectedly into sessions or technical meetings that involve long, complex discussions or being presented with documents that are full of jargon, not intended for business audience, that are hard to understand but still require their input. To the project, this may feel like it is the only way to get to the point where the requirements (and elements of the design) are complete, stable and agreed. Unfortunately, the transition from requirements (defined in business language) to the design (defined in technical language) can produce a barrier preventing the business from fully participating in these activities. In addition, the nature of the design work is that it is more detailed than the requirements. A single sentence in a requirements document may need a number of pages of design documentation, supported or elaborated via a set of complex diagrams and process descriptions, all of which will take much more of the business' time to consider and respond to than the original requirement would have done. The extent to which such additional consultation ends up being a burden for the business is not always appreciated by the project team.

There are also situations in which the project staffing for the design work may be different from the requirements phase. Project staff involved with requirements are likely to be closer to the business mindset than those involved with design, who are often more comfortable within their own technical discipline. This can widen the gap between the two worlds of business and project, and make working together during the design phase trickier than it was during the requirements phase.

There are situations where the business is required by the project to make decisions relating to the design (and sometimes the requirements) against quite tight timescales. At this point in the project, the project team starts to have more people on board and sometimes cannot make forward progress until a particular decision has been made and agreed. In the meantime, such individuals are in effect costing the project money but are not able to be as productive as the project would like. This can lead to the project team being quite blunt with the business about the importance and timescale pressure relating to the decisions that need to be taken by the business. The project may not appreciate the other activities which the business staff are engaged in and the constraints that this can impose upon their ability to make decisions within the deadlines demanded by the project. These demands for what the business may think of as unrealistic timelines for responses can start to have a negative impact on their day job and be a cause of some frustration.

BUSINESS LOCK-OUT

The design phase can be the start of a frustrating 'lock-out' for the business. This can continue through the build activities into the early testing work. The business may not be fully involved again until the test phase is well underway. Such a lock-out tends to occur on very sequential projects where once the requirements are settled and agreed, the project goes away to build what has been asked for and does so at arm's length from the business.

The risks associated with this include being unable to take account of changes in circumstances that mean that for legitimate reasons, the original requirements, although valid at the time, need to be amended and revised to take account of a new context and situation. In addition, questions may arise for the project that are not posed to the business, but instead the project makes a decision itself, which turns out to be incorrect, but which is only apparent when the eventual deliverables are tested by the business. Depending on the nature of the technical work within the project, the design and build phases can last a lot longer than the start-up and requirements phases. This means that the lock-out period can be quite substantial. Changes can happen within the business in terms of priorities, processes and staffing, all of which can mean that the business can lose interest in the project and give it less priority and focus. Any *esprit de corps* that might have been established can dissolve through neglect and reduced contact between the business and the project.

In summary, the design phase can represent that start of a frustrating time for the business and unless active steps are taken to minimise the impact of such frustrations, the situation can become quite unhelpful to the successful outcome of the project.

The Project Perspective

The project team can find the design phase equally problematic, although for different reasons. Some of these are the mirror image of the frustrations felt by the business.

NEW PERSPECTIVES

The bell curve of project staffing often takes a further ramp-up at this juncture. Design is the point where new members join the project team. They will have particular skills associated with translating requirements into designs. As such, they will not have been involved in the requirements work and they will need to come up to speed quickly. They will not have been exposed to the detailed discussions between the business and the project that led to the requirements, so the trade-offs, nuances of interpretation and subtleties of implementation will not be apparent to them.

This situation can have pros and cons. A fresh set of eyes can – if time is available and the designer has the inclination – question the assumptions that may be inherent in the requirements. This helps to validate that they are strong and robust requirements. In doing this, however, the new joiners can discover unexpectedly that some requirements are not deliverable. Assumptions may have been made that turn out to be unfounded. These assumptions may well have included that a particular requirement could be met with the available technology, tools, timescales and materials. The designers who are closer to how such solutions are built can bring some bad news to the project and as a result can cause it to have to revisit the requirements. Sometimes there may be more than one design approach to meeting a requirement, and as such the business's original objectives can still be achieved. Sometimes this can be done by the project in a way that is invisible to the business. In other situations, the original requirement, despite the best efforts of the project, just cannot be met. In this situation the project team will have to revert back to the business with the bad news. This can provide multiple impacts on the project as they will have reduced the confidence that the business team has that the project can be delivered as required, and because changes will be needed, almost inevitably costs will be increased. Although essential, the project–business exchanges about these requirements and design problems will introduce friction and provide an opportunity for a gap in confidence to open up between the two parties.

OUTSTANDING UNCERTAINTIES

One of the greatest difficulties faced by a project team covers the situation where there are both outstanding uncertainties and also a timeline that assumes that by this point in the project, everything is clear. This means that the project team is asked to keep pressing on with the design, even though certain key requirements are not yet clear, settled or agreed.

This is where a tension can develop inside the project team between the need to keep to schedule and the need to produce a design that meets the requirements and will be buildable. This scenario is quite common and the project and business working together need to find a way to deal with this situation.

GROWTH IN TEAM SIZE

As already mentioned, the design can often be more detailed and voluminous than the requirements, which can result in a step-up in team size. New joiners will not necessarily have full knowledge of the project's history and the business representatives, and so may be detached from the business perspective.

The project will have grown larger and the designers may interface with the requirements team inside the project rather than with the business team which helped develop the requirements. This is where misunderstandings can arise, as differing interpretations of a requirement can evolve as it is passed along the chain of individuals.

In addition, this is often the stage at which split-site working may occur. For example, in some types of project this could involve the design and development of a computer system by a team based remotely, even abroad. This introduction of new personnel remote from the core project team provides additional risks of miscommunication and as a result a design that no longer matches the original intent of the requirements.

Bridging the Divide

This chapter has discussed the challenge that faces a project when it moves into the design phase. In particular, this is when the risk of a gulf opening up between the business and the project really comes to the fore. To make sure that this is minimised and, if possible, completely avoided, a number of actions need to be considered.

CONTINUED BUILDING OF THE COMBINED TEAM

The addition of new resources to the project team at the start of the design activity, together with the fact that they may be geographically separate from the existing project and business teams, risks taking the whole business-project combined team backwards through the team formation lifecycle. Table 4.1 from Chapter 4 continues to apply, with the arrival of the designers potentially inadvertently disrupting what may be a 'performing' team.

Simply by recognising this, the project and the business can take action to make sure that the designers are brought rapidly up to speed with the

Initial team	F	S	N	P	P	P	P	P
Requirements experts		F	S	N	P	P	P	P
Designers			F	S	N	P	P	P

F = Forming / S = Storming / N = Norming / P = Performing

Table 6.1   Impact of types of staff on team performance

objectives, context and history of the project. Cultures always exist in projects, either being deliberately engineered or, in the absence of actions to create a specific culture, evolving haphazardly in something of a vacuum. The project and business therefore need to set and reinforce the culture of joint working, shared values and common vision that is needed to achieve success.

SHARED UNDERSTANDING OF THE DESIGN PROCESS

It can help immensely if the project is able to educate the business about how the project intends to do the design work, possibly by using case studies about how previous successful projects did their design. This can minimise the risk of misunderstandings and help bring everyone on to the same page. A particular element of this is to make the business aware of the preparatory work that may be required to ensure a good understanding of the 'as-is' situation before the 'to-be' design can be created. As organisations, business units and teams mature, a structural view of a business will tend to develop. For a project, there are times when a process view can be more helpful. A project seeking to change business processes will first need to establish what the current processes are; this will take time and as a result may feel like slow progress to external observers and sponsors. This is where communication between the project and the business can help.

SHARED UNDERSTANDING OF CHANGE

One bridge-building activity relates to setting the scene to minimise future business-project conflict. It involves ensuring that all parties gain a full appreciation of the cost impact of changes as the project moves through its lifecycle stages. In general the later a change is introduced into a project, the more it costs. Changing a one-line requirement during the requirements phase is easier and cheaper than changing a 30-page design specification, which in turn is cheaper than undoing a whole set of build activities which have already been implemented.

This means that there is significant benefit to the business and the project to get to a point by the end of design where all the requirements and the resultant design are complete, stable and agreed. This can impose an additional level of work in reaching agreement during the design phase, but if this agreement is not bottomed-out at this point, then changes that arise during the build phase will be much more disruptive and costly to implement.

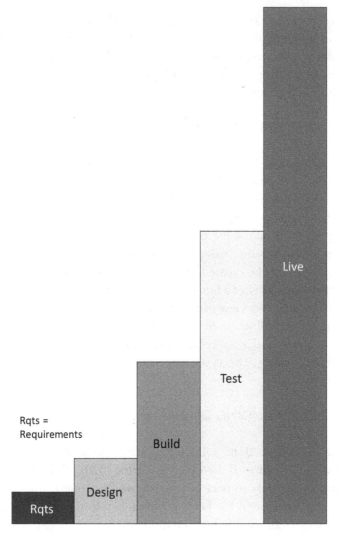

Figure 6.1   Cost of accommodating a change depending upon the phase when it is identified

As discussed earlier, the range of methods that can be used to make sure that all the design has been fully considered and all of its implications agreed include early demonstrations of the solution (where possible), process walkthroughs and general rehearsals of how the solution will work (sometimes known as table-top exercises).

Another key technique to assist with this is establishing a strong partnership between two very important roles known as the Business Authority and the

Technical Authority. The former knows how the business wants the project's deliverables to be put to use, while the latter knows how to build them. If the combined team is structured appropriately, then both individuals will have the necessary power and authority to arbitrate and take decisions so that the project is able to move forwards. For this to work well, effort must be put into creating a strong partnership between the Business Authority and the Technical Authority, so that they are motivated and incentivised to work together for the common good of the combined team.

There is a trend for organisations to develop a holistic view of how they operate, and one specialism that can assist with this is known as Enterprise Architecture. This builds a complete view of how a business combines its goals, how it operates, how it changes and how this is supported by technology, specifically information technology (Graves 2009). It usually does this using a suite of diagrams and documents. If the business is one that has an enterprise architecture already in place, then a way to reduce the gap is to make sure that the project is fully aware of this architecture and that the design that it develops complies with the business' enterprise architecture.

UNDERSTANDING THE IMPACT OF EXTERNAL STANDARDS

Projects that involve significant technical engineering may have to adhere to external standards that are not within their remit to ignore or vary. The degree of awareness of these constraints may vary between the business and the project. In some cases the business may include technical experts who specify the standards as part of the procurement process when engaging the project team, while in other cases the project team, notably the technical designers, will arrive with an understanding that of course these standards will have to apply and will presume that the business is aware of this. In each scenario the application of these standards may come as a surprise to one or other party. Including joint discussion of all applicable standards and their implications early in the design review meetings will be the best way to reduce the levels of surprise and make sure that they are applied intelligently, with knowledge and insight, and where possible their interpretation is tailored to fit with the needs of the business and project.

AVOIDING ELABORATE DESIGNS

Both the business and the project need to take care that as the requirements are translated into the design, an over-engineered or excessively elaborate design is not created. Projects tend to develop a momentum of their own and can result in a scenario of the 'tail wagging the dog' when they create designs that are too complicated. This can happen as a result of either good intentions: where the project designers have a strong eye for detail and can be overly perfectionist and want to do a really proper job of the design occasionally they can also arise as a result of poor intentions where a supplier (who is being paid on a T&M basis) attempts to string out the work for as long as possible. In both situations the end result is a design that is more complicated than is necessary, which will take more time and money to build and test, and may prove to have been the wrong solution. A key question to ask when reviewing the design deliverables is therefore whether a simple process change might be enough to get the most of the desired benefit without the need for the more elaborate design.

Key Points

- The design phase of a project can be where a shift in emphasis emerges with the focus of the project moving from the business team across to the project team.

- This change, particularly with the introduction of more technical language, is one of the first steps in a journey which can disenfranchise the business.

- The levels of technical complexity associated with the design stage can make the activity incomprehensible to the business.

- Any overhang from the requirements activities can lead to business team members being involved in technical meetings that involve long, complex discussions, or being presented with documents that are full of jargon but still require their input.

- Project staff involved with requirements are likely to be closer to the business mindset than those involved with design, who are often more comfortable within their own technical discipline.

- The design phase can be the start of a frustrating 'lock-out' for the business. This can continue through the build activities into the early testing work.

- For the project, design is the point where new members join the project team. They will not have been involved in the requirements work and they will need to come up to speed quickly.

- The project team may face a situation where there are both outstanding requirements and design uncertainties, and also a timeline that assumes that by this point everything is clear.

- As the project grows larger, the designers may interface with the requirements team inside the project rather than with the business team which helped develop the requirements.

- This is often the stage at which split-site working may occur.

- To bridge the divide, both parties need to understand the points made above and consider the following:

    - Continued building of the combined team. The addition of new resources to the project team at the start of the design activity, together with the fact that they may be geographically separate from the existing project and business teams, risks taking the whole business-project combined team backwards through the team formation lifecycle. Active steps need to be taken to avoid this.
    - Establish a shared understanding of the design process. It can help immensely if the project is able to educate the business about how the project intends to do the design work, possibly by using case studies about how previous successful projects did their design.
    - Also establish a shared understanding of the impact of change on the project. This involves ensuring that all parties gain a full appreciation of the cost impact of changes as the project moves through its lifecycle stages – in particular, that the later a change is introduced into a project, the more it costs.
    - Consider the necessity of adhering to external technical standards, which may only become apparent with the arrival in the project of technically skilled designers who take this for granted, whereas it may have been overlooked until now.
    - Avoid elaborate designs. Both the business and the project need to take care that as the requirements are translated into the design, an over-engineered or excessively elaborate design is not created.

Chapter 7
Build

The Business Perspective

The build phase of the project can, from a business perspective, actually be the part of the project that makes most sense. The preceding phases relating to getting started, identifying requirements and undertaking design can appear as a rather laborious preamble to really getting on with the proper project, which from a business perspective involves the creation of the deliverables required to make the solution happen.

IMPACT OF PROJECT TYPE

The build phase of a project can be radically different depending upon the type of project. This will have a consequence for the actual and perceived level of business involvement that will occur during this phase.

The key determinant of the type of project relates to the attributes of the solution, specifically the tangibility of the deliverables. This can range across quite a number of scenarios:

- Physical construction.

- System build.

- System configuration.

- Organisational change.

- Mergers and separations.

PHYSICAL CONSTRUCTION

Physical construction is in many ways the easiest for the business to appreciate. If we are talking about some sort of building or civil engineering work, once the initial groundwork or foundations are complete, then the rate at which the building progresses beyond that tends to be very evident. In addition to being visible, the progress is often quite easy to appreciate, e.g. the rafters but not yet the tiles are on the roof, so the building is not yet watertight. This type of deliverable, which the business can see and touch, means that progress is clearly obvious.

SYSTEM BUILD

System build, which involves the construction of a computer system, can be far harder for the business to assess in terms of the build progress. The technology may not necessarily be particularly accessible or understandable. Even if it is familiar to the business, there may be layers of it which are similar to physical foundations – which are needed before the main application can be built – but not visible in any meaningful way to the business. The upshot of all of this is that there is a real risk of the business feeling locked-out or excluded from the build activities, and only becoming involved again when the finished article is presented as ready for testing.

SYSTEM CONFIGURATION

Some system development is subtly different, from a business perspective, in that it involves making changes to an existing computer product – known as configuration. This means that there may be some halfway-house in that the unconfigured version of the product can initially be shared with the business. Depending upon how the software product is set up, it may be possible to do so in stages and let the business see how the configured product is evolving. This will reduce the risk of lock-out, but may have the unintended consequence of bringing forward a problem that would otherwise only surface during testing. This is when the business, finally seeing the software system in action, realises that what is being provided is not quite what was wanted. Knowing this sooner rather than later may well be a good thing, but it could disrupt the build if at this stage checking back against the agreed requirements is needed, followed by re-working of the designs and the building of a new configuration.

ORGANISATIONAL CHANGE

Organisational change projects can be far less tangible. At one level, they are very paper-based, with their main deliverables being items such as new organisation charts, job descriptions, communications plans and similar items. Until the button is pushed and these changes are actually put into effect, there will be no real noticeable delivery. The speed of the changes when they do happen can also vary greatly – some all come into force overnight on a particular date, while others may be spread out over several months of consultation. The softer aspects of the change, where cultures are developed and new loyalties are established, can take a lot longer and are also difficult to measure in terms of whether they have actually delivered what was intended.

MERGERS AND SEPARATIONS

Mergers and separations are a different sort of organisational change. They tend to involve a lot of paper-based legal due diligence, again making the process more difficult to track. The financial and legal transactions that result in the buying or selling of companies, or the legal structures needed to establish or close down public bodies, tend to be extensive, complex and sometimes hard to track. Many documents will go through numerous iterations of review and comment. The extent to which the business has visibility of these will vary according to the culture of the business and the way in which the technical experts (such as lawyers and financiers) choose to involve the business. Levels of business comfort and confidence will therefore also vary quite considerably.

COMBINATIONS OF SCENARIOS

In a significant number of projects, more than one of the individual scenarios mentioned above may exist. There are occasions where most of them will apply, maybe at different phases of a project. In such cases the comprehensibility of the project's build activities to the business will be reduced by the complexity of the changes and the fact that some of the more visible areas may be reliant on some of the less visible types of deliverable.

TECHNICAL DETAIL

In general the business will have an expectation that the project knows what it is doing. That is why the business arranged for people skilled in project work to undertake this rather than using day-to-day staff. The project up until this stage may have found it convenient, and the business may have also wished that technical details were left in the hands of the project as much as possible. Based on the presumption that all will go well, the business does not want to be needlessly distracted with large amounts of technical detail. As an analogy, most aeroplane passengers would rather not have all of the flight dials and read-outs displayed to them on their inflight movie screen, but tend to be quite happy with a simple progress indicator showing where in the world the airplane currently is flying and how long before it reaches its destination.

Projects, however, can run into technical problems. Sometimes even with the best will in the world, these would not have been evident until the build work actually got started. Where this arises, there can be a degree of impatience within the business if there are detailed technical problems that are not explained well. The business presumption tends to be that 'this stuff ought to work' and therefore why is the project 'making a mountain out of a molehill'. The technical build staff on the project, although understanding the problem best, may be the least well-equipped to explain it clearly to the business, and as a result may overplay the problem, or alternatively under-estimate its significance to the business.

TEST PREPARATIONS

During the build phase, the business may be requested by the project to become involved in preparations for validating or testing that the deliverables will meet the agreed requirements. To ensure that no time is lost, this test preparation activity often happens during the latter stages of the build phase, so that the testing can then follow on seamlessly at the end of the build.

This requirement for validation and testing input can come as a surprise and a burden to the business. If it was not included in the plans, or was included but was not communicated clearly enough, then the business may not be in a position to keep its side of the bargain. The business activities can include approving the tests, assembling test data andmaking business people available to assist with user-level testing. Finding the right people at the right time is not always feasible for the business. They may be too busy, there may be particular seasonal demands on their time and they may need training in project requirements and/or testing techniques. This can leave a sour taste for the business as this unexpected demand upon it will either not be able to be met, thus delaying the project, or will be met, but as a result other areas of business activity will suffer. In either case a further wedge will be driven into the gap between the business and the project.

The Project Perspective

The build phase presents the project with a major challenge. This is where all of the requirements and design, which up to now may well have only been in the form of documentation, is now turned into the actual deliverables for the project. As discussed above, these can range from physical buildings and engineering products through to software, process, organisational or legal changes. What is significant is that this is where they are actually built, developed, constructed, assembled and got to a state where, provided they pass their validation and testing, they can be used.

The previous sentence, '… where they are actually built', makes the whole build process sound very straightforward, but in reality this is where the project faces a significant challenge. The building activity may be inherently difficult and tricky, it may require very finely tuned tools or it may be novel and never have been attempted before. It may be well understood, but whatever the case, it is very rarely as straightforward as the plans would suggest, as the business would expect and as the project team would hope. Whatever the nature of the project, something unexpected can derail the carefully laid-out plan, the highly choreographed build steps, the intricately sequenced series of incremental creation and construction activities.

In some cases it may be problems with the processes to be followed – the processes were not well-enough thought through – or they may have included assumptions about how the build should be done that turn out not to be achievable. In other cases there may be problems with the inputs to the build process, errors in the design, poor-quality input materials that form the start of the physical construction process, missing detail or overlooked decisions – whatever it is in practice, the effect is the same.

This is not pessimism but observation borne of experience. It is in the nature of projects to experience surprises during the build phase, sometimes predictable (if effort were put into forecasting earlier), sometimes totally unforeseeable. Whatever their nature or cause, they do just tend to happen. This is what makes experienced project managers seem more cautious than the business might expect when this stage is reached. There is the useful feature that the progress is much more visible to the business, but this is also akin to working in a greenhouse under strong arc-lamps; any hiatus in progress, any problem meaning that the construction or creation activities need to be put on hold whilst the problem is fixed, is highly visible to the business, and as a result the project can feel more vulnerable than it did in earlier phases.

NEW STAFF AND MORE STAFF

The project is now an established entity with its own culture, momentum and history. However, the build stage can herald another multiplication in the number of staff working on the project. For every requirements writer, there may have been three designers, while for each designer, there may be 10 builders. In this example, the project, which had two requirements authors, now has 60 builders. The exact numbers are not critical – what is important to appreciate is the potential scale of the ramp-up in staff.

Such growth can be difficult to achieve smoothly and quickly. The nature of the build might mean that a lot of build tasks can be done in parallel, but finding enough suitably skilled builders, all available at the same moment, all able to be on-boarded at the same time and all equipped with the relevant tools and infrastructure, may stretch the project too far. Under these circumstances the project may be forced to make compromises in terms of how quickly it can get up to full build staffing levels and therefore how quickly it can in practice move forwards. Experienced project teams know this and plan accordingly, but it can come as a surprise to the business, which may not have given this much consideration.

The arrival of these new staff will yet again cause an evolution in the culture of the project team. There will be a new tranche of workers who are not familiar with the history and context of the project. They will be coming into the project raw, fresh and focused very much on the build tasks at hand. In terms of style, they may be deep technical specialists, experts in building the deliverables required, but not necessarily that interested even in the processes for managing the project, let alone the impact that their deliverables will have on the business and how the business will put them to good use. This is not deliberate ignorance, it is simply a byproduct of the division of labour that is necessary to set up and run a project as it moves through its phases. There is, however, a consequence to this, in that these new staff can alter the centre of gravity of the project team, dragging the project view closer towards the technicalities of the build and further away from the hopes, desires, culture and expectations of the business.

THE EXISTING STAFF

The project will now have been running long enough for some of the early joiners in the project team to have moved on to other work. Sometimes this is because their expertise is no longer required, as the project has moved to a new phase; in other cases this is simply due to the highly dynamic world of projects, which often sees project specialists moving from project to project, organisation to organisation, and not always at the end of a project, but quite often midway through if the career path for them is more attractive elsewhere.

This attrition in experienced members of the project team can by the build phase start to pose a problem. Depending upon the culture and style of the project, there may be certain crucial aspects of the project that do not exist on paper, but in the heads and collective memories of the key players. Risks start to rise with the turnover in project staff meaning a key loss of knowledge of what has happened so far. Important agreements can start to be lost or forgotten if they are not properly recorded.

The collective culture can also change as staff leave the project. In particular, if the earlier stages of the project have faced difficulties, this can sometimes be the point at which additional senior project management resources are brought in either to strengthen or completely renew the project management team. This can reinvigorate a project, but it can also lead to a loss of shared knowledge and experience, and the culture and team development needed to be able to function effectively may need to be re-created.

DELAY COSTS

With the numbers of staff involved in the build phase, the impact of a delay can be pretty significant for the project team. If there are a large number of highly specialised individuals or expensive equipment being hired and if a problem means that a sequence of activities needs to be put on hold whilst the problem is resolved, then the costs of having the staff or equipment idle can very quickly mount up. Projects done by separate organisations, where the project team is selling its services to the business, only proceed if the project is very competitively priced. This means they have a tight profit margin, which can easily be wiped out in such circumstances. If the project team is inside the business, then the additional costs being incurred will probably end up being passed on to the business and can turn a financially sound business case into one that no longer makes sense; in the worst-case scenario, the project needs to put a lot of effort into making sure that costs do not spiral up and extend a long way into the future.

As a result of this risk, all projects are particularly focused – almost obsessively so – on identifying and tracking issues that arise during the build phase and getting them resolved, even in quite a rough way, as soon as possible so that forward momentum can be maintained.

CHANGE COSTS

The other area of costs that a project can fear relates to change. If the project has made it all the way through start-up, requirements and design, and has started to actually build deliverable, then if it now discovers that some of the deliverables need to be changed, it is faced with much higher costs. What has been built may have to be discarded completely; it may be partly salvageable and be able to be re-worked; or it might have to be dismantled to then form the start point for a new deliverable. Whatever happens, this is not good news for the project. The costs associated with all of this will be significant, since all of the earlier phases will need to be revisited – leading to adjusted requirements, amended designs, and new plans and schedules. Whilst this analysis work is being done, parts of the project team may be on hold and some tasks will certainly need to be repeated. This will all have serious cost implications, which will play out similarly to those discussed in the section above, depending upon the nature of the project–business relationship and the commercial structure. But, however it is structured, at the end of the day, extra work will need to be done. In some cases, physical material that was acquired will not be used and not included as part of the final deliverables.

MULTIPLICATION AND MAGNIFICATION

The other challenge faced by the project is that rarely do the problems of the build stage come along as one-off events. There are normally a range of problems and often some of them will happen at the same time. Their interaction, and knock-on effects on each other, will have a compound effect, and as a result they will magnify the overall challenge and costs faced by the project.

The result of all of this is that the project team during the build phase will end up very 'heads-down driving for the line', with a strong focus on achieving delivery. This may seem almost insensitive to the business viewpoint, but without this single-minded determination, the project faces a real risk of being knocked off-course as it undertakes the trickiest phase of its lifecycle so far.

Bridging the Divide

To close the gap between the business and the project when the build phase is reached, one of the simplest and most effective techniques is for each party to put itself in the other's shoes for a moment. If the project can realise that for the business, by now things must be quite frustrating as only now is it seeing something actually start to be delivered, and, likewise, if the business can appreciate that the project is now faced with the difficult challenge of actually creating the deliverables, which up to now have just been discussion points, then both sides will be able to gain a little more insight into where the other party is coming from and what feelings may drive their behaviours during this phase.

It is also worth remembering that this phase is potentially one of the longest phases, particularly when it includes the early stages of validation and testing, which are done by the project team rather than the business. This can leave room for a chasm to slowly open up without the parties necessarily realising that they are getting further apart. To avoid this happening, a variety of practical and pragmatic techniques may be deployed.

MEASURING THE BUILD PROCESS

Where possible, it can be helpful to devise ways to measure the build progress. The first step in this is to decide what constitutes a sensible 'unit of build'. For a tall building, it would probably be a completed floor, for a software system, it might be a screen, while for a new way of working, it could be a fully defined process description. Whatever it is, this needs to be agreed upfront between the business and the project so that when it is used to report progress, both parties have confidence that they attach the same interpretation to it and that it is the robust measure of progress that they find useful and meaningful.

This build metric can then be used to track detailed performance against forecasts. It should be possible for the project and business to jointly agree a forecast rate of build, such as two screens per week or one floor a month, so that once the build has gotten underway, the actual performance can be compared against a shared expectation of how the build was expected to progress. If the build runs into problems, then the focus can be given to the underlying causes and how to recover from the problem, rather than on spurious disagreements prompted by the alternative ways of measuring and tracking the build rate.

INCREMENTAL DEMONSTRATIONS

Where the nature of the solution allows it, a related approach is to make sure that there are incremental demonstrations of what has been achieved to date. Something physical can be inspected, a building site can be visited and a software system with a number of functions may be able to have the early functions demonstrated to the business. This can help to build confidence on both sides. The business starts to see that the project is making real progress and that what it asked for is actually what is being developed and will be delivered. Meanwhile, the project gets to know that the business has seen what is being created and is comfortable with it.

There will inevitably be comments and feedback, some of which might prompt a change of course or adjustments to what is being built. The protocol for such incremental demonstrations therefore needs to be worked out and agreed in advance. Depending upon the nature of the project and the build process, it may be necessary to make clear to the business that they can inspect, but at this stage not request changes. In serious situations, if such a demonstration highlights that a change is essential, a formal change control procedure will need to exist and be followed. For other types of project where the build can be more flexible and take account of evolving business feedback, such rigidity on commenting may not be required. Such projects are sometimes known as agile (Beck et al. 2001).

There need not just be a single demonstration – the active word here is incremental. It may well be possible for the business to witness the creation process at a number of junctures. Each step in the build process that results in a new demonstrable deliverable will give the business greater confidence that the project is on the right track. This may feel like an unwelcome distraction to parts of the project team, particularly those who would rather work undisturbed and uninterrupted, and deliver a complete finished working article. If the project management can get the buy-in of such builders to this demonstration activity, then they may find that it actually makes their lives simpler in the end, as the business – when it subsequently comes to validate, test and accept the deliverables – will already be familiar with them and potentially be better disposed towards them. This can lead to a smoother and more successful acceptance stage.

DRY-RUNS OF PROCESSES

Whatever the nature of a physical deliverable, it is very unlikely to sit in splendid isolation without some human use of some sort. This will almost always be in the form of a process of some nature.

Whilst the build is progressing, in parallel with the actual build, this phase of the project is the right time to start to walk through or dry-run the processes that will be needed to make use of the deliverables. In essence the solution will be a combination of the deliverables and the processes. It is likely that by this stage, the business will have started to identify the people who will be involved in performing the processes once the solution is actually in use. This is now the opportunity for the project to work with them to try out the processes and, as a consequence, make sure that they are realistic, workable and fit well with the deliverables that are being created. This future facing joint working can help concentrate all the minds in the joint team on their shared goals and outcomes. By working together in this way, getting to know each other and targeting effective realisation of the solution, the teams stand a better chance of creating a successful result.

ACTIVE STAKEHOLDER MANAGEMENT

There may also be a wider range of more remote stakeholders who over time have lost touch with the project. This phase is also the time to rekindle that relationship, and use the joint project and business team to reach out and explain the solution and its creation to these stakeholders. The business and the project will come closer together if they have to act jointly and collectively engage with a number of separate third party stakeholders.

SHARING CONCERNS

The project team may, if it feels sufficiently comfortable, try sharing some of its risks and concerns with the business. This sort of frank disclosure may feel odd and that it is putting the project at some sort of disadvantage, but in doing so, the project can build trust with the business, which will help strengthen the working relationship.

An example of this relating to the build phase would be a situation where the project includes novel technology, or even the novel combination of pre-existing technology, as this will be riskier and less predictable than the implementation of existing well-proven technology. To deliberately highlight this to the business means that the project is treating the business as a sensible adult. The business is made aware of the risks that are inherent in this particular type of build activity and if problems do arise, they will come as less of a surprise and let-down, and the business may be more inclined to take a constructive route to helping resolve such difficulties.

Key Points

*   The build phase of the project can from a business perspective actually be the part of the project that makes most sense.

- The build phase of a project can be radically different depending upon the type of project: physical construction, system build, system configuration, organisational change, and mergers and separations.

- In general the business will have an expectation that the project knows what it is doing. The business can be impatient if there are detailed technical problems that are not explained well. The business presumption tends to be that 'this stuff ought to work' and therefore why is the project 'making a mountain out of a molehill'.

- A requirement for business input to the validation and testing can come as a surprise and a burden to the business. If it was not included in the plans, or was included but was not communicated clearly enough, then the business may not be in a position to keep its side of the bargain.

- For the project, the build phase presents a major challenge. This is where all of the requirements and design, which up to now may well have been only in the form of documentation, is now turned into the actual deliverables for the project.

- The building activity may be inherently difficult and tricky, it may require very finely tuned tools or it may be novel and never have been attempted before. It may be well understood. Whatever the case, it is very rarely as straightforward as the plans would suggest, as the business would expect and as the project team would hope.

- The project is now an established entity with its own culture, momentum and history. However, the build stage can herald another multiplication in the number of staff working on the project.

- The project will now have been running long enough for some of the early joiners in the project team to have moved on to other work. Risks start to rise with the turnover in project staff meaning a key loss of knowledge of what has happened so far.

- With the increased numbers of staff involved in the build phase, the impact of a delay can be pretty significant for the project team.

- If the project has made it all the way through start-up, requirements and design, and has started to actually build deliverables, then if it now discovers that some of the deliverables need to be changed, it faces much higher costs.

- Rarely do the problems of the build stage come along as one-off events. Their interaction, and knock-on effects on each other, will have a compound effect, and as a result they will magnify the overall challenge and costs faced by the project.

- To bridge the divide, both parties need to understand the points made above and then:

  - where possible, devise ways to measure the build progress;
  - where the nature of the solution allows it, arrange incremental demonstrations of what has been achieved to date;
  - this phase of the project is the right time to start to walk through or dry-run the processes that will be needed to make use of the deliverables;
  - for the more remote stakeholders who over time have lost touch with the project, this phase is also the time to rekindle that relationship;
  - once the build has been completed, the project will then move into the validation and test phase.

An antagonistic relationship between the project and the business can be seriously exacerbated during the test phase. So let us know turn our attention to that area and how to minimise the level of conflict involved.

Chapter 8
Validation and Test

The Business Perspective

Validation and testing can be very complex, with the earlier steps in the process not particularly visible to the business. The nature of the testing will vary depending upon the type of solution that the project is delivering. However, in almost all cases there will be a series of stages. These multiple stages of validation and testing activity can be confusing from a business perspective. It is perfectly possible that there may need to be:

- testing of individual units;

- testing of the integration of units to create a system;

- testing of the system as whole;

- testing of how the system integrates with other systems in its wider environment;

- testing of the non-functional attributes of the solution; and finally

- acceptance testing by the business of the solution and how it will operate in practice.

From a business viewpoint, this can all seem quite excessive. Surely if it was built properly, it should work?

It is also quite common for the business and the project to come to the validation and testing process with opposing viewpoints. The validation and testing phase brings to light a fundamental difference in philosophy regarding testing – for the project, the aim of all the testing (except the final acceptance testing) is to uncover errors and find all of them, so that the solution is error free. A good test finds an error, so it was a good use of time and effort, since not everything can be tested and therefore testing has to be selective. The business wants to see the solution demonstrated as working; a test that shows a problem or error is not good news, it undermines confidence – what else might be wrong? It introduces uncertainty into the timescales for when the solution will be ready to go live. This difference of perspective can set the tone for misunderstandings during all of the testing activity, apart from the final acceptance tests.

The start of the validation and test phase may coincide with a spectrum of outcomes. At one end of the spectrum, it may be the first time that the business has come into contact with the project for quite a while. If this is the case, there is a real risk that the business may discover that what is being delivered does not match what was requested. Clearly the other end of the spectrum is much better, whereby the business and the project have kept in close touch and tracked both the creation of the deliverables, and also the evolution of any changes that were needed to be made. In this second case the risk of surprises is obviously much less, and so the gap between the business and the project should be much smaller, if it exists at all.

Therefore, the main scenario of concern is the first one. If the business has been shut out from the design and build work, then it may have lost touch with what was asked for and may no longer be in a position to properly determine whether what is being provided matches its needs.

The business, if it was separated from the project, may not have communicated to the project that the world has moved on in the intervening period, and so what was requested is now no longer what is needed. This realisation, when confronted by deliverables, which although asked for are now no longer what is wanted, can cause significant problems. The business will be faced with a decision as to whether to reject the solution and ask for it to be re-worked to match the new situation, which is likely to cause the project to impose additional costs on the business, or to accept the solution – in part or maybe in whole – with the consequence that it may have to either adjust its expectations or ways of working to be able to make use of what has been created according to the original requirements.

Half a step before this realisation comes the actual activity of validation and testing. What this means for the business will of course vary quite considerably, depending on the nature of the solution that is being delivered – for instance, physical, software or process. Some physical edifices will simply need to be inspected, other engineering and software products may require active testing by the business, processes will need dry-running, while other types of deliverable can only be reviewed and then accepted (e.g. a legal document) and then, once it is signed, action taken.

The level of business involvement in this validation and testing activity may come as a surprise to the business. If the relationship between the business and the project is weak, strained or hostile, then the business may not have had adequate forewarning of the extent to which the project needs the business to contribute to the validation process. This demand for business resources to assist with the tests may therefore be unexpected; even if anticipated in principle, it could also be too great in number, and in particular it may not fit in with business calendar. There could easily be peaks of activity which coincide with the scheduled validation and testing activities. If the tests were to happen at a different time, the business might be able to provide enough resources to enable the tests to happen, but otherwise if they are to happen as scheduled, the business faces having to make a compromise. Should it damage its day-to-day activities by taking people away from its peak load work, so that they can do the test, or should it use fewer resources on the tests, thus reducing the rate at which the tests get done and so delaying the date for go-live? This could be quite costly in two ways as the project would then last longer and cost the business more; in addition, if the solution is meant to save the organisation money (which is quite likely as otherwise the project probably would not have got approval to go ahead in the first place), then the savings will be realised later, with an additional cost being entailed by having to wait longer for the savings to start.

The business may under these circumstances be tempted to reduce the amount of validation and testing. This may superficially seem appealing. The wisdom of this will depend upon the criticality of the solution that is being delivered, that is, the consequences of it not working properly or failing once it had gone live. For some situations, this may not have major consequences, while for other solutions upon which life and limb depend, such an outcome would be unthinkable. So the risk appetite of the business combined with the nature of the solution will set the scene for whether it is possible to cut down on the testing or not.

The actual testing will vary in nature, as mentioned above, but in particular for certain types of solution, there will be a need to validate the process elements of the solution in some depth. This is likely to involve activities such as dry-runs or service rehearsals. Such activities may need to involve staff who will be new to the business and engaged specifically to be part of the new solution. The situation can arise where these new staff may not yet be in place or, even if they are, may not be sufficiently briefed or trained to be able to start to do the tests when the schedule requires. This is not always the fault of the business – it may have known about the need for the extra staff and have planned in a sensible lead-time for their recruitment, but unexpected market conditions may have caught the business by surprise and caused the recruitment process to take longer than expected, leading to a shortfall when they are required by the original schedule.

Testing is often organised into cycles of tests. This involves running a set of tests, with the expectation that some may need to be repeated. This is fine provided that both the business and the project fully understand and buy into this approach. However, slippage due to timescale challenges and possible earlier problems in design and build could mean that there is only enough time available to do one cycle of testing. A presumption may develop within the business that all the tests will pass successfully. Problems necessitating fixes and retesting will at this stage impact on the schedule and thus cause much wider impacts, which again will seriously damage business confidence.

If the project is fortunate enough to have time for multiple cycles of testing, the business will still need to be briefed on how this operates. As mentioned earlier, the idea of doing tests, looking for and, in the early cycles, expecting failures, fixing the problems and then re-doing tests may strike the business as excessive, pessimistic or unambitious.

The earlier stages of technical testing are often carried out by the project team, since it is not directly related to the business and tends to require very specialist technical knowledge. As a result, the business may be excluded from these stages. However, if such testing does not go smoothly, news of problems uncovered may start rumour mills and lead to worry about the project within the business.

The business itself is not necessarily a single cohesive organisation. As the project reaches the validation and testing phase, schedule pressure will be getting greater. With the live date approaching, there can be a greater risk of slippage and failure. This can lead to a potential loss of face within the business in terms of the relationship between the members of the business, who are directly responsible for the project, and the senior management to whom they report. This can put surprising levels of stress on the business team and can cause what may seem to be small problems which people would normally treat as little local difficulties to be magnified disproportionately, resulting in significant acrimony between the business and the project.

If there are testing failures and problems during the acceptance testing activity which completes the validation and testing phase, then the business is likely to experience a very real drop in confidence. This may be disproportionate to the nature of the test failure and the implications it has for the solution, but nonetheless the level of satisfaction that the business feels with the solution can be significantly dented.

The Project Perspective

Now we turn to the project viewpoint. For the project team, validation and testing is often the most stressful part of the project. The nature of the work in this phase means that there will often be long hours, combined with late notice of unexpected scheduling and rescheduling of time and activities. When test items that were expected to pass do not pass, they need correcting and then re-testing.

For the project, as emphasised earlier, the initial focus will be on finding problems and removing them. This is often done in an iterative way. A successful early test breaks the deliverable. It is deeply embedded in the project psyche, particularly for test team members, that it is better to find the problem now than later when the solution is in active use.

Testing can involve another change in project personnel. One of the key tenets of strong approaches to validation and testing is to use a separate team. Everyone takes a certain level of pride in their work and it is very hard to do a volte-face and attempt to look for problems in what you have created. Good tests often attempt to break a deliverable, particularly a software product. This can also apply to a hardware product where it needs to be confirmed that the item will meet the stresses and demands placed upon it. Again the project can be faced with challenges relating to how this influx of new team members will affect the overall dynamics of the team. By the time the validation and testing phase has been reached, time will be particularly tight, and getting these new staff recruited and fully set up so that they can get started with effective testing as soon as possible will be quite a pressurised activity.

It is rare that the project team is composed of people who are all from one organisation. In many cases there will be a set of suppliers, maybe a single chain, maybe a network fanning out to include a variety of suppliers probably with a range of geographical locations. The requirements that the business gave to the project will have gone to the project team at the top of the supply structure and then subsets of these will have been passed down the chain to the various suppliers. Each internal relationship in the project customer–supplier hierarchy to some extent mimics the relationship between the business and the project. This means that the project team will want to do some sort of validation and acceptance testing on the deliverable components that are being supplied to them by the next-level-down supplier.

This pattern can in turn repeat itself for a number of layers depending upon how long each of the internal customer–supplier chains is. The result is that the validation and testing activity that the project has to do can be considerably more complex and extended than the business might expect when treating the project as a 'black box'. At each step in the chain, the same set of considerations and risks apply, so that any deliverable component that fails validation and testing will need to go back to the relevant supplier for re-work and fixing.

The upshot of all of this is that it is very hard to predict when testing will be complete. A considerable amount of planning effort will be invested by the project team into getting the validation and testing activity clear, sequenced and controllable. However, because it is not possible to predict which tests may fail, it is not possible to cover all contingencies in terms of how the validation and testing activities will work out in practice. Until the deliverables are free of defects that will prevent the business from using them, and therefore mean that they are not going to be accepted, the project will need to continue with the iterations of 'test – find problem – fix – retest'. There are occasions when fixing one problem can sometimes introduce other problems, which may not always be spotted straight away. This means that the validation and testing phase can often feel like 'two steps forward, one step back'. Project teams who have gone through this a number of times before will recognise this scenario and will mentally factor it into their expectations of how the validation and testing will unfold. There is as a result some inherent realism on the project side, which can result in a mismatch of viewpoints compared to the business, which may be assuming a more successful outcome and may find the project's realism more akin to pessimism.

The combination of the two considerations relating to a scenario where a project has a network of suppliers and where testing highlights deliverable problems, necessitating re-work and re-testing, is exacerbated when the network is taken into consideration. Timescale pressures often dictate that a project plans its activities, including validation and testing, so as to maximise

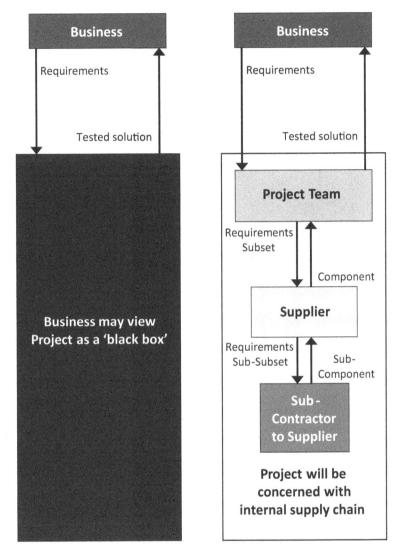

Figure 8.1   Black-box and supply chain views of project testing

the number of parallel activities and achieve the earliest possible completion date. A problem with one sub-supplier's deliverable can potentially hold up a number of other sub-suppliers and cause a much greater knock-on effect than might be expected considering the defect in isolation. In summary, with this complex network of suppliers, producing deliverable components that other suppliers depend upon, the overall progress of the validation and testing activity for other suppliers and for the overall project team is much less predictable than the business might hope.

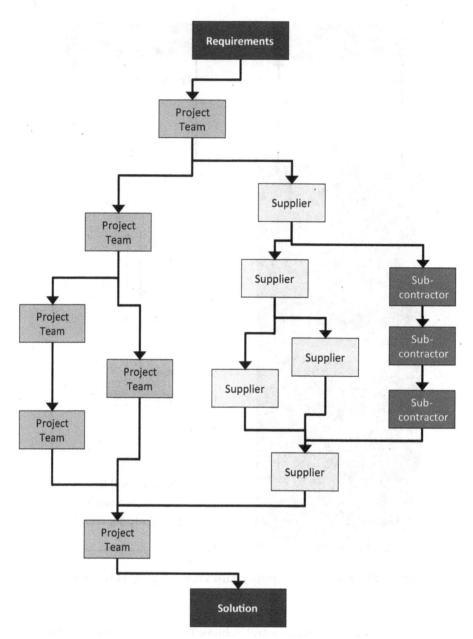

Figure 8.2   Parallel working by project suppliers

As the project's validation and testing activity nears completion in terms of the internal testing, it shifts across to focusing on achieving acceptance of the deliverables by the business. This is where the mindset of the project team needs to change, as at this stage the emphasis is now on a demonstration that the project deliverables provide the functions or services that were requested. For testing staff who are schooled in the mantra that a 'good test is one that finds an error', this can be a bit problematic and their natural style can come as a surprise to the business.

This can be the point where a project team that has focused on the technology of the solution, without getting a proper handle on the business process, both current and new, will now face great problems when it comes to achieving acceptance, and may find that it has delivered the wrong solution.

The management of this acceptance stage needs careful planning and execution, as it involves a mixture of project staff and business staff. The exact arrangements can vary in terms of who reports to whom, and this can lead to misunderstandings, clashes and turf wars in relation to getting the team set up and staffed on a continual basis. One of the great frustrations for the project is where it finds that, although it agreed a level of business involvement in the testing, potentially only a few months ago, when it comes to the actual testing, the business is no longer able to make the required individuals available. There may be clear and pressing reasons from the business viewpoint as to why the resources need to attend to other work, but often the project finds that the business does not fully appreciate how disruptive this unavailability can be to the timely completion of the acceptance activities. The worst-case scenario here is where the business resources, who were involved in the requirements and therefore are best placed to judge sensibly whether the deliverables match the requirements, are not available and alternative resources, who do not properly understand what is required, are provided instead.

Another problem can arise when the set of validation checks and acceptance test cases that need to be followed have not been fully reviewed and agreed by the business in time for the start date of the validation and acceptance activity. This can be due to a variety of causes – for example, the tests may have been developed late by the project and provided to the business only just before the start of the acceptance activity. Alternatively, the project may have provided the tests in good time, but the business may not have got the relevant knowledgeable and skilled staff to focus on the tests due to either overlooking them or the pressure of other priorities. The extent to which this can be avoided and resolved often rests with whether the business–project relationship is strong enough for the project to place tasks and expectations on the business in a similar fashion to the way that the business will give tasks to the project.

Bridging the Divide

Central to minimising the divide during the testing phase is careful groundwork, with a focus on strong partnership and effective communication. During validation and testing, whenever errors are uncovered that show a mismatch between the solution and the requirements is when the most friction can arise between the business and the project.

This is so crucial that it is worth re-emphasising. Validation and testing is where the 'rubber hits the road' – if it is a shambles, with lots of failures emerging, the inevitable tension between the business and the project can lead to rapid escalation of issues towards senior levels of management. If problems race up the organisation structure too quickly, then a breakdown of relations can ensue. Once trust and effective working relationships are damaged, they can be difficult to repair, especially during a phase that is often as tense as validation and testing tends to be. To try to avoid this, multiple levels of communications and multiple channels of messaging are needed. These can be enhanced by using an 'authority level' concept whereby items are targeted for resolution at a particular level in the structure, and should only move further up the hierarchy if the scale and significance of the error merit it. That way, senior management are only involved if the problem is so serious that no one below them in the hierarchy can resolve it.

Business	**Project**
Project Sponsor	Head of Project Organisation
Client for Project	Project Manager
Business Requirements Author	Chief Designer
User	Project Team Member

Table 8.1   Example of levels of communication during testing

There is a particular type of problem that validation and testing can uncover. If a project has an extended duration, the environment around it may have moved on. The originally agreed requirements, although being fine when first settled, may now no longer be appropriate. It is possible that no one has realised this in the intervening period, and only now does the validation and testing finally uncover this. There can then be a clash between the business and the project because it may not be clear what the best thing to do is. The project could go ahead and go live with the old requirement, which is what was originally asked for, and keep close to the original schedule and live date. Alternatively, a time delay can be taken so that the deliverable is changed to align with the new requirement. This can have a major impact with change assessments, redesign of the solution, rebuild of the deliverable and re-testing of other parts of solution, together giving a significant cost and schedule impact. Arguments can often ensue in terms of whose 'fault' it was that it was not found or realised sooner. This often then boils down to who pays, which, in turn, does not help with a harmonious relationship.

The end of testing is sometimes difficult to establish, as there will usually be a number of outstanding concerns and problems. The business and the project need to work together to determine which of these are show-stoppers that must be resolved before the solution can be put into live use and which can be tolerated with waivers or workarounds, either indefinitely or for a limited period of time.

The previous establishment of agreed protocols for how to handle validation and testing will smooth this 'have we finished yet?' activity. Otherwise the two parties may well be pushing for contradictory outcomes. The business will not want to go live until as few problems as possible remain, whereas the project will want to wind down as soon as possible so that it may well attempt to sell a problem or two as not being really significant and try to persuade the business to live with the problems. Rarely, the reverse positions may arise, whereby the business has a fixed deadline and may want to get the solution into operation before it is complete, stable and ready to go; likewise, the project may wish to string out the testing, particularly if it is being paid using a T&M approach. If the business is employing an independent specialist to run the testing on its behalf, then such an individual may be motivated to push for the testing to continue for as long as possible, since they will continue to get paid, and they may choose to portray this as making sure that the solution really is tested as thoroughly as possible. All of these potential scenarios for disagreement about when to stop testing therefore justify the effort that needs to be put in at the start of the testing phase in order to agree the mechanisms for running and controlling the activities of the phase. This means that good decisions can be made which are not excessively clouded by partisan interests and exacerbated by tired and exhausted testers arguing with exasperated and disappointed business representatives.

Eventually an agreed conclusion will be reached, at which point the business and project will jointly accept that the solution, with whatever problems may remain, is in fact good enough to be put into use and go live. This will be the topic of the next chapter.

Key Points

- Validation and testing can be very complex, with the earlier steps in the process not particularly visible to the business.

- From a business viewpoint, this can all seem quite excessive. Surely if it was built properly, it should work?

- This may be the first time that the business has come into contact with the project for quite a while. If this is the case, the business may discover that what is being delivered does not match what was requested.

- The business, if it was separated from the project, may not have communicated to the project that the world has moved on in the intervening period, and so what was requested is now no longer what is needed.

- The level of business involvement in the validation and testing activity may come as a surprise to the business.

- With the live date approaching, there can be a greater risk of slippage and failure. This can lead to a potential loss of face within the business in terms of the relationship between the members of the business, who are directly responsible for the project, and the senior management to whom they report.

- The business wants to see the solution demonstrated as working – a test that shows a problem or error is not good news, it undermines confidence.

- For the project, the aim of all the testing (except the final acceptance testing) is to uncover errors and find all of them so that the solution is error free.

- For the project team, validation and testing is often the most stressful part of the project.

- Testing can involve another change in project personnel. One of the key tenets of strong approaches to validation and testing is to use a separate team. Everyone takes a certain level of pride in their work and it is very hard to look for problems in what you have personally created.

- The validation and testing activity that the project has to do can be considerably more complex and extended than the business might expect, particularly if there is a long supply chain involved.

- It is very hard for the project to predict when testing will be complete.

- The project team can sometimes focus on the technology of the solution without getting a proper handle on the business process, both current and new. The team will now face great problems when it comes to achieving acceptance and may find it has delivered the wrong system.

- Problems can arise when the set of validation checks and acceptance test cases that need to be followed have not been fully reviewed and agreed by the business in time for the start date of the validation and acceptance activity.

- To bridge the divide, both parties need to understand the points made above and then:

  - focus on strong partnership and effective communication;
  - use an 'authority level' concept whereby items are targeted for resolution at a particular level in the structure and should only move further up the hierarchy if the scale and significance of the error merit it;
  - establish agreed protocols for how to handle validation and testing so as to help with answering the 'have we finished yet?' question.

Chapter 9

Going Live

The Business Perspective

Going live is seen as the culmination of everything that the project has been working towards. Putting the solution into operation represents the realisation of the vision for the business. But going live can have many shades of meaning depending upon the nature of the solution and the deliverables. It is sometimes a single point in time, while in other situations it is more like a start to a series of activities. For an office block, it might be the first occupant moving in, but not the last as it may take a number of months for all the floors to be let and occupied. For a bridge, it would be the first vehicle driven across by a member of the general public. For an IT system, it would be turning the system on and the first user logging in. For a new business process, it would be the first set of inputs transformed using all of the steps, resulting in the expected output. For an organisational change, it would be the 'vesting day' when the new organisation officially takes over, has all of its powers and authorities, and has the staff all in place.

One key feature of this point in the project is that this is where, metaphorically speaking, the keys get handed over. Sometimes this happens for real. The significant aspect of this is that the focus of power, ownership, control and action, which for many months (and maybe years) has been with the project team, moves back to the business. The business, which might have felt that it was the junior partner in terms of actually getting things done, moves back into the ascendancy. This can be quite a challenge and an eye-opener, since habits of thought and behaviour that will have built up over an extended period of time are now swept aside and the roles reversed.

This is a critical moment for the business. Having completed the validation and testing and assured itself, to the maximum extent possible, given the constraints of time and budget, that the solution meets its requirements, it now has to 'throw the switch'. This is often far more public than the preceding phases, so that if it were to run into problems, there would be 'egg on the face' of the business for all to see. This means that the business will tend to be quite careful about how this process is actually undertaken.

Things will vary depending upon whether the solution is implementing something brand new that has not been in existence and operation before, or whether it is taking over from something that already exists:

- In the first case, the reliance on testing is in a much greater, as there is no guarantee, other than the validation and testing, that what has been developed will actually work in practice in the real world with the planned volume of users/items/clients when it is operating at full capacity. The consequences of it going wrong would vary depending upon whether it was safety critical, highly brand sensitive or not. In some situations it would be possible to return to the status quo ante of not having the solution, and wait for it to be fixed and then made available again. In other situations this might be disastrous and therefore, as well as having the proper solution, a set of fall-back arrangements would also need to be ready to be invoked.

- In the other case, where the solution is replacing something that is already in existence, the challenge is different. Even if the new solution works, the previous situation gives a reference point against which the it can be compared. Stakeholders will vary in their approach to such comparisons, some perhaps highly logical, others more emotional, some fair and balanced, others jumping to conclusions on limited evidence. What will be certain, however, is that the new solution will be on trial for a while, until the users are convinced that it is an improvement on the situation that went before. Interestingly, the existence of a previous solution does at least provide in most cases some protection to potential problems with the new solution, since the business can hopefully switch back to the old solution and use that again until the malfunctioning new solution is fixed and available.

There can be a change of staffing on the business side. This point is often when higher-level management, who may have taken a back seat whilst the project was deep in design and build, make a comeback. Their presence is very valuable in demonstrating that the business is fully behind the solution that the project is delivering. Where projects need to achieve cultural and behavioural change in order for the solution to be successful, the backing of senior management can be key to success. However, their background, probably quite separate from the project and potentially much more involved in the regular heartbeat activities of the business, means that the project and its concepts and practices may be more of an alien environment to them. This may come as a surprise to the project team, who by now would expect everyone in the business management hierarchy to fully understand not only what the project was delivering, but also how the project has been working and what the obligations are on the business to make sure that the project's deliverables are successfully put into live operation.

Before the go-live can happen, there is often a need for quite extensive final checks. These are separate from the validation and testing that confirm that the solution is acceptable. They are more to do with making sure that every small step in the cut-over process of moving from the 'before the solution' world to the 'solution is now running successfully' world have been identified, checked and performed. This is a mini-project in itself, but comes with a complication, because many of these final check and set-up tasks will need to be done by people from the business. Therefore, the same considerations relating to business staff, who are unfamiliar with projects, apply to this stage. Very often there is a fixed and well-published go-live date. When this is the case, a head of steam builds up and the date becomes fixed in many people's minds. The public commitment to go live on this date means that it becomes not only a 'line in the sand' but actually 'carved in stone'. As a result, the date, even if it is movable, becomes for all practical purposes, immovable. This means that the set-up tasks need to be micro-managed down to the deadline as if certain of them are missed or go wrong, the project may miss the target date. This active micro-management can feel unfamiliar and uncomfortable for the business, but is perfectly normal for the project team. This can lead to a mismatch in expectations in terms of what it is reasonable to expect the business staff to do to achieve go-live and how they should be managed during this process.

Rollback plans are often needed and are a sensible professional precaution. Where business staff are not used to this, they can be surprised that these are being put in place – 'Does the project not have enough confidence...?' – so their creation and potential implementation needs to be communicated in an effective way, otherwise this can lead to an inadvertent and unintended loss of confidence by the business.

A further subtlety to this is that for some projects, there will be a point of no return. In certain situations this will be the moment of go-live. In other cases it may be sometime after initial go live when a critical mass of actions, data or people is now involved, and the previous arrangements cannot be reinstated. For others it may also be after go-live, when a previous arrangement is decommissioned and cannot then be put back into use. The involvement of the business is central to making sure that this point – sometimes more than one point – is identified and fully planned into the schedules.

With the business view on going live clarified, before the project can actually push the button, we need to examine the contrasting viewpoint of the project team. Both the business and the project are working towards the same goal, but potentially with different concerns and areas of emphasis.

The Project Perspective

The project viewpoint on going live can be more complex and nuanced than the business viewpoint. This reflects the fact that the project has a fuller appreciation of the nature of the deliverables that it has just provided and what needs to be done to turn them from a set of deliverables into a successful working solution. In addition, project teams have often gone through many go-live situations before, whilst this may well be the first time for a significant number of people from the business.

From the project viewpoint, go-live may actually be somewhat different from a business perspective. The moment the solution is made available for use, it can be said to have gone live. There will need to be all of the support structures and arrangements fully in place. However, the actual usage of the solution may not happen immediately. The 'open for business' moment may happen at a weekend (deliberately so) and in practice the solution may just 'sit there and hum' until Monday morning when the users of the solution actually start to put it to work. This gives the solution a chance to warm up and bed in before being subject to the full loading of usage. There may be a different sort of uptake whereby usage increases gradually over time; this may be because the solution, although built for a particular volume of activity, can only ramp up to this level of business in a series of gentle steps. The ramp-up may occur not because of system constraints, but due to the level of availability or enthusiasm of the user community, who may not all rush at once to start making use of it.

One other dimension of spreading-out a go-live may relate to functions, teams or geographies. The solution may be complete and ready to roll, but due to constraints from either the business or the project (or both), it may not be possible to put it into action everywhere at exactly the same time. This can result in a phased approach, with a range of options, including turning it on for use everywhere but gradually phasing in its use, or turning it on in stages per location or function. Again, this will to some extent blur the line in terms of whether go-live has or has not fully happened.

Whatever the cause of the gap or delay in reaching full capability, the resultant gap will nonetheless lead to a difference in perception between the business and the project. The project will be of the opinion that it has discharged its obligations if the first users have started to make use of the solution, i.e. at the start of the ramp-up activity, whereas the business may well consider that go-live has only really properly happened when all the users have made use of the solution and it is running at full capacity. This can affect when the project thinks it ought to get paid for a successful go-live and when the business thinks the project actually deserves to get paid.

Another focus of the go-live will be the stopping and turning-off of preceding solutions. If the solution is replacing an earlier solution (i.e. it is not part of creating a brand new function that never existed before), then the earlier arrangements will need to stop. In some cases the deliverables and the solution will have a monopoly on providing a particular outcome or service, for instance, an air traffic control computer – two competing systems running at the same time controlling the same airspace would not be wise. In this situation the old system will have to stop being used, and in some cases information in it transferred seamlessly and in a very timely fashion into the new solution. Once this has happened, the change to the new solution then becomes almost irreversible. In other situations it may be possible to run two approaches side-by-side. This is sometimes done to make sure that the new solution is running correctly, to phase it in and to provide a fall-back arrangement in the event of problems, which can be put into action quickly and easily. This means that the project will devote a certain amount of attention to getting the existing arrangements shut-down and handed-over in a very carefully controlled way. This may surprise some people within the business, who will be more focused on what benefits the new solution will bring and how to get it quickly into use. This can lead to a clash, because these shut-down tasks quite often need to be done by people from the business, over which the project may not have as strong control as it does over members of its own team. Again, frustration and annoyance can ensue if both parties do not realise why the other side is behaving in the way that seems sensible to it.

Significantly, once the project considers that go-live has happened successfully, as well as celebrating, and maybe breathing a sigh of relief, it will also start to wind down almost immediately. The staff on the project will depart quickly, as the tasks left for them to do rapidly diminish. They hold the knowledge of the project, and unless this is well documented, as they go through the door, the knowledge goes with them. For the project, this quick wrap-up is common practice and the business may at a superficial level welcome it as it will signal the end to the large costs that may have been incurred until this point. However, the rapid departure of most of the team can also go relatively unnoticed by the business if it is mainly focused on getting to grips with the new solution. It may be a short while – when things have bedded-in and are in starting to feel like the 'new normal' – that the business can suddenly realise that most of the project team is no longer there. This could take it by surprise and if there were any final areas that the business needed attending to, any other handover information or confirmation of detailed support arrangements, all of this may be asked for too late with no one left to deliver it.

Bridging the Divide

The go-live moment, being the most public part of the project's delivery, is one where a united front presented by both the business and the project to the rest of the world is highly advantageous. So, what needs to be done to keep the two parties together at this penultimate phase of the project?

To achieve the best outcome for the go-live process, it is crucial that everybody needs to be together in terms of deciding whether the situation is right for go-live to happen. This will require quite a substantial series of meetings. Depending upon the degree of partnership or animosity, there may be a benefit in using a neutral party or a facilitator to ensure that these meetings run smoothly and are productive. The earlier the decision process for moving to go-live can be mapped out and agreed, the better. This will be because there will probably be less baggage on both sides and a positive and constructive approach can be taken to agreeing the process. With the process settled, when it comes to actually making the decisions, the process simply has to be followed. There may be disagreements about whether the solution is ready for go-live, but there will not be additional arguments about whether the way in which the go-live decision is being made is the right approach. The tricky point here is that attempting to map this out in some detail, reasonably far in advance of go-live, can be hard. Both the business and project will be more focused on the other tasks in hand, and people tend to be comfortable focusing on detail in relation to activities that are close at hand. Micro-planning an activity that may not happen for a number of months can feel like overkill and a distracting waste of time when there are other more pressing matters to attend to. Nonetheless, if enough discipline to undertake this can be mustered, then the eventual go-live decision-making process will be much less fraught.

For the go-live process to succeed, two areas need to be addressed:

- painstaking planning; and

- continual communication.

PLAN FOR THE WORST, HOPE FOR THE BEST

The planning of the go-live needs to take the project and the business, in parallel, through a series of states detailing how things will be hour-by-hour in the run-up, during and immediately after the go-live. For some types of solution, this may just be the 24 hours either side of a well-defined single go-live event, while for other situations, this level of detailed planning could need to extend backwards for weeks before go-live and similarly forwards. The granularity of the scheduling and tracking of events will vary with how close they are to the go-live point. Months out it might be daily, weeks out hourly, and for the closest few days maybe by the minute. This may feel like overkill, but this is one of those situations where it is better to be safe than sorry. Using this template can prompt thinking of actions and events that might otherwise have been overlooked, and in the end, if it turns out that a slightly less detailed analysis will be adequate, at least this method will have forced the thinking process and have resulted in a deliberate decision to choose the right level of granularity for the planning.

IT'S BETTER TO OVER-COMMUNICATE THAN RISK BEING OVERLOOKED

A general feature of lives in the twenty-first century is that they are almost always far too busy. As a result, attention spans tend to be limited, be it at work or at home. Many people fight a bit of a losing battle with their emails, voicemails and to-do lists. As a result, people tend only to have the personal bandwidth to deal with the important and the urgent. Everything else is either ignored from the start, or receives only momentary attention and so is soon swamped and overlaid by something more pressing or critical. This means that the messages that all the participants in the go-live process need to receive, understand and act upon are competing with a plethora of distractions that reduce the likelihood that they will hit home. The range of participants who need the communication covers the complete set of project and business team members, plus more senior management, and any other groups who may be classed as 'users' of the solution but are not part of the business.

The painstaking planning that has already occurred needs to be augmented and extended with a further strand of analysis, identifying which messages need to be created and transmitted, and to whom, across the same timeline as the actions in the plan. The underlying assumption within this also needs to include the fact that only a proportion of the messages will get through and register with their target audiences. This means that the same message may have to be delivered a number of times and in a variety of formats and mechanisms. Steps may need to be included to check and confirm that the recipients of the messages have registered them, understood the communication and, where they need to take action, are aware of what this action is, when they need to do it and have the motivation and necessary equipment to enable them to do so.

Multi-zone or multi-department business clients will complicate all of this. Rolling out a solution to multiple elements of a federated organisation over which the centre does not have command and control will provide a difficult business challenge as uptake has to be voluntary or else highly incentivised.

One other aspect that may get overlooked, but is needed for the go-live to work, is to consider any support functions within the business that look after the type of technology or arrangements that form part of the deliverables. These existing 'business as usual' support functions may suddenly get an extra set of deliverables, systems, processes or data that they need to support. The new deliveries from the project, as well as being used, will now also need to be supported and maintained. This will add an extra set of tasks to the workload of this team. Some tasks may be the same as they already do, but others are likely to be somewhat different. Forgetting to include this part of the business in the planning for the go-live will have consequences that could hit the solution sooner rather than later. They need to be factored into the final steps of validation and testing, so that the business can be confident that not only will the solution work on day one, but that it will continue to work for the whole of its planned lifetime. This leads back to the communications challenge – this group must not be overlooked and these support functions are sometimes spread across quite a wide-ranging organisational landscape – they all need to be considered.

Finally, there will need to be a long-term home identified to hold the project knowledge so that it is not lost when the project team departs. In a similar fashion, the shadow business team may well also disband. This may take a while longer, but sometimes since the business team has a more informal structure, it can dissolve without anyone realising this is happening, and then suddenly one day it is realised that there is no one left in the roles they had when the project was happening, and knowledge is rapidly evaporating. Only if there is an organisation-level function to capture, catalogue and curate knowledge will the good work of the project be properly preserved.

Key Points

- Going live can have many shades of meaning depending upon the nature of the solution and the deliverables.

- The focus of power, ownership, control and action, which has been with the project team, moves back to the business.

- This is often far more public than the preceding phases, so that if it were to run into problems, there would be 'egg on the face' of the business for all to see.

- There can be a change of staffing on the business side. This point is often when higher-level management, who may have taken a back seat whilst the project was deep in design and build, make a comeback.

- Before the go-live can happen, there is often a need for quite extensive final checks.

- Rollback plans are often needed and are a sensible professional precaution. Where business staff are not used to this, they can be surprised that these are being put in place.

- For some projects, there will be a point of no return.

- Project teams have often gone through many go-live situations before, whilst this may well be the first time for a significant number of people from the business.

- From the project viewpoint, the moment the solution is made available for use, it can be said to have gone live. However, the actual usage of the solution may not happen immediately.

- The project will view that it has discharged its obligations if the first users have started to make use of the system, whereas the business may well consider that go-live has only really properly happened when all the users are making use of the solution.

- Another focus of the go-live will be the stopping and turning-off of preceding solutions.

- Once the project considers that the go-live has happened successfully, it will start to wind down almost immediately.

- To bridge the divide, both parties need to understand the points made above and then:

  - it is crucial that everybody needs to be together in terms of deciding whether the situation is right for the go-live to happen;
  - the earlier the decision process for moving to go-live can be mapped out and agreed, the better;
  - plan in detail for the worst, but hope for the best;
  - it is better to over-communicate to all the categories of team member and stakeholder than risk the go-live planning messages going unnoticed;
  - identify a long-term home to hold the project knowledge so that it is not lost when the project team departs;
  - present a united front to the rest of the world.

Chapter 10

Post-Live Realisation of Changes

The Business Perspective

Go-live has now happened, 'so that's it, we're done' – not so fast. Parts of the business may assume that because the solution has now gone live, the project is over. This will not always be the case. For some projects, which deliver a highly technical solution, the creation of the solution will mark the end of the project. However, for other projects, where the objective is to change the way an organisation functions, the technical deliverables may be a necessary enabling factor, but in themselves they do not constitute the complete solution. For the project to successfully achieve the objectives set for it, the changes that need to accompany the now-operational technical deliverables also need to happen. This is not necessarily straightforward.

The timescales for these changes would appear to need to be as soon as possible, but there are variations to this that will depend upon the nature of the changes and how quickly the organisation can adopt the technical solution and adapt its way of thinking and working.

What might these changes be in terms of the business? There may be changes that mean that staff can be released from old roles. The business is faced with the question of how and when should this happen. This partly depends upon whether the old roles have in effect converted into some new equivalent role, which the staff can still do but may need to be retrained to perform. Alternatively, the old roles may have been completely abolished and subsumed into the system, meaning that the staff are unfortunately surplus to requirements unless there is some other activity that they can undertake. This may be similar in terms of nature (with transferrable skill-sets) – e.g. moving from one sort of customer support to another. These sorts of changes do not happen overnight and benefit from considerable pre-planning. The staff will need to receive significant amounts of communication ahead of the changes if they are not to become demotivated. Some may not like the change, may see the writing on the wall and may leave the organisation to find a new position elsewhere. This may not be what the business wants, as retaining these people would keep valuable knowledge within the business, but to do so will take active support and engagement, following on from the initial communication, so as to build their confidence and faith in the future that it would be worthwhile for them to stay with the organisation.

Whatever happens, there are likely to be non-trivial costs. If staff remain and need to be retrained, this will cost money. If staff leave, there will be departure packages that the business needs to provide. Either way, as part of the overall project and business activity, the business should have factored in these costs; however, they may come as a late surprise if the business and project teams were focusing mainly on the tangible project deliverables.

Having made the organisational changes and started working with the new business processes, the business will now be expected to demonstrate that the project was worthwhile. As part of the project, the business will have put in place – if it was not there already – a method to quantify both how much the project cost, but also how much less the business is needing to spend now that the project has been delivered. This will be discussed in more detail in Chapter 16. However, the challenge that the business will face in moving from the go-live activity into the post-live changes realisation activity is that although it can now start to collect data to demonstrate that the project has hopefully made a change that will save money, it may take some time for this evidence to appear. A variety of factors can affect this.

The financial timeline can run into the future with a number of financial years needed to fully assess the changes. There may be a requirement for evidence that the benefit has bedded-in and therefore lasted. As a result, the business may be faced with keeping a function in place going forward for some significant period of time in order to make sure that the changes have happened, have stuck and have made a difference. The members of the business team close to the project, who know the detail of what needs to change, how long it will take and what will be needed to prevent the business slipping back into its old ways of working, will understand this. The senior business management who are more distant from the project may not appreciate this to the same extent. They could well be more impatient for results and want to declare victory. The business could find that it is forced to forecast future victory on the basis of relatively scant early evidence, which it is then committed to make happen.

One other complication that can befall the project at this stage is what may have happened in parallel in the real world whilst the project was getting on with designing and creating its deliverables. It is quite possible – indeed it is more likely than not – that the shape of the business will have changed. The context and landscape, the structure of the organisation, the nature of the services provided, the functions undertaken – any and all of these may now be different from when the project started. As a result, it might not now be possible to realise the originally intended benefits. This can come as a surprise to all involved, as it can get overlooked during the focus on the project. The business will then be faced with the challenge of making the best of what the project has provided and attempting to recoup its costs in some way or other.

What is significant in all of this is that the timescales may be much more extended than they were in the project. The wave-front of change may also be much wider, a large number of people, in many parts of the organisation, potentially spread around the world, all needing to change and adapt to the new capabilities offered by the project. Getting this to happen will take positive effort. It is not just a byproduct of turning the solution on. The business may not realise that this level of effort is needed and it might fall to what remains of the project team to prompt the business about this and get it started on the right path. This can be a real challenge for the project, as by now there really will be very little of it left. So what of the project team's viewpoint?

The Project Perspective

For the project team, the situation is rather different. A few of the team may have some tangential involvement in the post-live realisation of the changes to the business, but for most, this will not be uppermost in their minds. For them the project is winding down and is in effect over. Most of the project team will have rolled-off, some quite a while ago, but now certainly only a few senior roles will remain filled, together possibly with some communications and business change specialists.

The way that the project team judges the success of the project will differ markedly from the business perception. Its focus will be upon the three classic goals of time, cost and quality.

TIME

Time will be the most obvious goal in terms of whether the project delivered to its original stated deadline. There will be potentially differing viewpoints on this between the project team and the business. If there were agreed changes to the scope and deliverables during the project that affected the end date and pushed the go-live date further along, then provided that these were agreed and signed off, the project team will consider that if the revised go-live date was met, then they will have succeeded. However, depending upon what was promised to whom originally and how public the pronouncements were about the original target go-live date, the business may still harbour disappointment that the original date was not met. This will feel odd and unfair to the project, but nonetheless can set the tone for discord.

If the project has over-run and a revised date was never formally agreed, then once go-live has finally been achieved, the project is likely to be extremely relieved, whilst the business will be frustrated and disappointed. A harmonious end to the project is unlikely.

In the rare event that the project was delivered early, everyone will tend to be very happy, although if the project team was being paid by the day and as a result its income is less, it may not be as content as the business might expect it to be.

Time is generally simple to measure, although multiple go-lives in different locations can muddy the waters, particularly if some go-lives are achieved on time and others run late. Even so, there is in general an agreed yardstick against which all of this can be measured – the calendar.

COST

Cost will be trickier for the project and business to agree on. It is extremely rare for a project to have no changes and to run to the exact predicted effort levels that were identified at the start. The viewpoint on cost will vary depending upon whether the project was fixed price or T&M, and of course whether the observer is in the project team or the business.

For a fixed-price project, the project team will have had a lot of pressure put on it not to over-run. If there have been changes to the scope where additional finance was not secured, then the chances that they needed to do extra unfunded work will have increased. Similarly, if there have been significant problems with the design, build and testing of the solution, then the amount of effort required to meet the agreed requirements (even if these have not changed) would still be more than forecast, and could easily push the project into a loss. Other circumstantial problems could also have resulted in financial difficulties; if the project had made assumptions about how quickly and easily it might have recruited the necessary technical specialists, only to find when the time came that they were not easy to obtain and would cost a lot more than budgeted, then again the project might be pushed into a loss. All of these situations mean that the management in the project team would be viewed by their senior management as having failed to some degree or other. If they were having to report financial status on a regular basis, which is what would normally be expected, then they would have experienced significant stress to minimise the loss and to attempt to bring the project back into profit if at all possible. As a result, the project's staff are likely to have been under considerable pressure and strain from their own senior management, in addition to whatever pressure the business was putting on them. This will all colour their view of whether the project was a success or not from a financial viewpoint. In contrast, the business will have insulated itself from cost-shocks by working on a fixed-price basis with the project team. A strong project team will have conducted robust negotiations with the business to ensure that a narrow interpretation was taken of any ambiguous areas in the requirements, so as to minimise the scope of the delivery, which could have left a sour taste with the business due to the project being more combative that it might have expected. However, apart from this, the business will tend to be quite happy with a fixed-price project, as it will have obtained its solution for the initial agreed price without any nasty surprises in terms of additional costs. The only caveat here is that if the supplier was screwed down too tightly, although it may have been able to deliver the project, this may have been a very tight call. With only just succeeding, the loss to the project team's organisation could be significant enough to affect its viability. As a result, the project organisation that may well be needed to provide ongoing support for the solution may cease trading as the losses become too heavy to bear, which then leaves the business rather cut adrift on its own without the ongoing support it expected.

By contrast, if the project was a T&M deal, then the boot is very much on the other foot. The project will have been more relaxed about its finances, knowing that in principle all of its costs will be met by the business. There may, however, have been more antagonism and clashes between the project and the business during the lifetime of the project, as the business may have felt that the project was behaving as if it had been given a blank cheque. The business will have wanted a much greater level of visibility of costs and progress, as the eventual cost to the business will have been far less predictable. This will have put a greater workload on the project in terms of reporting progress and costs to the business, but even so, unless the business had at some point reneged on the deal to use a T&M approach, the project would in general have been far less stressed, and in all cases would have been able to claim some sort of financial success.

QUALITY

The project and the business perception of quality may well differ. The project's viewpoint will be centred around whether the requirements were met. If the validation and testing exercises successfully demonstrate that this was the case, then as far as the project is concerned, it will have met its quality goals. The business may take a softer, wider and more considered view of the quality situation. Different stakeholders will have varying perspectives and their judgements will change over time, as they get used to the solution, as it beds in and as it becomes part of normal working life.

For the members of the project team, this can all be too late, since they will want to be off to get started on the next piece of work, either for the same business or maybe a completely different client. They cannot afford to wait around to see if the quality has been declared as being achieved many months later. The only other thing which they may want, which will hinge on the quality dimension, is some sort of reference or testimonial from the business, which they can use to help them secure additional work in the future. The willingness or otherwise of the business to provide such a reference will provide a sharp insight into whether the viewpoint on quality of the business and the project do in fact coincide.

The final consideration of the project team, once everything has been wrapped up, will be, depending upon the arrangements between the business and the project, the provision of warranty and support for the solution. Where support is needed, scope can develop for confusion and misunderstanding at this point. Early support calls may not run as expected. Support will not always be required, but, where it is, there can be scenarios in which some of the project team remain in place for a long time supporting the live solution, they may even transfer into the business to perform this task or, alternatively, the project may use another part of its organisation to provide the support. In this case the handover from the project to the support organisation, although potentially not that visible to the business, will still need to be done in a smooth, controlled and comprehensive way, otherwise the problems with the subsequent support may undo all the good delivery work done by the project and over time may unjustifiably tarnish the reputation of the project's deliverables.

Bridging the Divide

At this stage the divide between the business and the project may matter less. However, both parties would prefer to feel good about the project and the achievement of its objectives rather than want to be involved in a failure. By working together to make sure that the post-live changes that are needed to achieve the intended objectives for the project actually happen, both parties will be in a better position to leave the endeavour with their heads held high.

The first area that needs to be addressed is the realisation of benefits. It is quite possible that the members of the project team may wash their hands of trying to realise benefits. They may think that the aim of the project is to create the ability for the business to realise the benefit, but that it is up to the business to make the relevant organisational or process changes. The business may disagree and can be faced with a situation where the business can have no one in the 'shadow project' who has this responsibility or skill.

So, although this may be the strict interpretation of the agreement between the business and the project, it can be to the project's ultimate advantage to bend and flex a bit and to come to the assistance of the business with this final task. The challenge facing the project if it chooses to do this is to make sure that it has individuals with the right skill-set to enable this to be done. These people may not have been involved in the technical build, and will instead need a combination of consultancy skills and knowledge of the sector that the business operates within and how it runs. A joint team, with this skill-set from the project together with resources borrowed from the business, can give the business team what it needs to be able to make the changes that are required.

In undertaking this work, the joint team will need to face a number of considerations that can provide a challenge to getting the change to happen.

Selling changes to working practices to the business will be difficult if the changes are not aligned to their needs and suitably incentivised. The joint change team may find that only now do the full ramifications of the intended changes become evident. The scale of the change required, the number of people who have to do things differently, the degree of discretion that they have over whether or not they choose to change and the urgency with which they think it is worth their while changing will vary quite considerably. The change team will have to find ways to get inside the heads of the business, and maybe users and consumers, and determine what will motivate them to change. A voluntary change that people buy into tends to be more effective and stick better than a change that is imposed and mandated.

The change team may come across the classic 'law of unintended consequences', which claims that for every designed change, somewhere else a balancing unintended change will arise that can have negative consequences that may outweigh the positive intention behind the original change. That is perhaps a bit over-dramatic, but it does make the point. Quite often when the project introduces a change that solves someone's problem, it inadvertently makes life different and maybe harder for others. If this is the case, and it is realised by the rest of the business and ecosystem, then the change will not easily be adopted in the business. To address this, ideally the project and the business should have modelled the whole of the business at the start so as to identify what the knock-on effects would be of the planned change and sought agreement from the other parts of the organisation ahead of getting going with the project. Such involvement early on could lead to redesigning elements of the deliverables and solution so as to minimise these expected knock-on effects. If this engagement happened, then the senior management elsewhere in the business could then be enlisted at the post-go-live stage to support the change and help their teams come to terms with whatever residual knock-on effects still remain.

Once the project and business working together have achieved, to whatever extent possible, the required post-go-live changes, the focus will then turn to formally determining the extent to which the project was (or was not) a success. This will vary significantly depending upon the viewpoints of the various stakeholders, which can be quite contradictory.

Key Points

- Parts of the business may assume that because the solution has now been put live that the project is over.

- For projects, where the objective is to change the way in which an organisation functions, the technical deliverables may be a necessary enabling factor, but in themselves they do not constitute the complete solution.

- These sorts of changes do not happen overnight and benefit from considerable pre-planning.

- The business will now be expected to demonstrate that the project was worthwhile.

- The business could find that it is forced to forecast future victory on the basis of relatively scant early evidence, which it is then committed to make happen.

- Whilst the project was getting on with designing and creating its deliverables, the shape of the business may have changed and it might not now be possible to realise the originally intended benefits.

- Realising the benefits will take positive effort; it is not just a byproduct of turning the solution on.

- The way that the project team judges the success of the project will differ markedly from the business perception.

  - Time will be the most obvious criterion in terms of judging whether the project delivered to its original stated deadline.
  - Cost is trickier for the project and business to agree on; it is extremely rare for a project to have no changes and to run to the exact budget set at the start.
  - The project's viewpoint on quality will be centred around whether the requirements were met. It cannot afford to wait around to see if the quality has been declared as being achieved many months later.

- Problems with subsequent support may undo all the good delivery work done by the project and over time may unjustifiably tarnish the reputation of the project's deliverables.

- To bridge the divide, both parties need to understand the points made above and then:

  - work together to make sure that the post-go-live changes that are needed to achieve the intended objectives for the project actually happen;
  - it can be to the project's ultimate advantage to bend and flex a bit and to come to the assistance of the business with this final task.

- be aware that selling changes to working practices to the business will be difficult if the changes are not aligned to its needs and suitably incentivised;
- the change team needs to be ready to address manifestations of the classic 'law of unintended consequences';
- the project and the business should work together to formally determine the extent to which the project was (or was not) a success.

This leads us to the end of the project lifecycle, but not the end of the consideration of how business and project teams can work more closely together. In addition to the phases that a project goes through, there are also a set of common practices or strands of activity that are undertaken throughout the duration of a project.

These strands of activity cut horizontally through the lifecycle and can have just as much of an impact on widening or closing the gap between the business and the project. The latter part of this book now discusses these areas in greater depth.

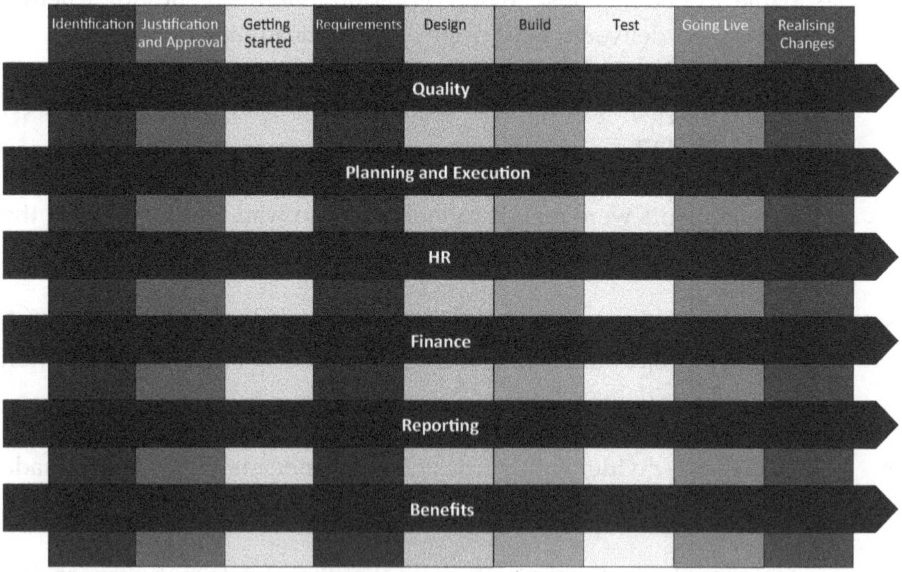

Figure 10.1   Lifecycle phases and activity strands

PART II
Common Strands

Chapter 11
Quality

There are a number of common strands that run through a project from start to finish and they can be discussed in a variety of orders. I am placing quality first, as this remains central to my view of what projects are created to achieve.

The Business Perspective

From the viewpoint of the business, quality can be a bit of an enigma and a surprise. The enigma relates to how it can actually be quite difficult to tie quality down. The surprise is due to how a project can turn out in ways that the business did not expect, and in particular at a level of quality that was not anticipated.

Quality is in the eye of the beholder and, more practically, the experience of the user. It can be very subjective, depending on the nature of what is being created by the project. If it is a single item, of which there is only one, it will be possible to specify its attributes and features, and then measure them at a later date to see if it met the requirement. Provided that this requirement did in fact capture the quality expectations of the business, a quality solution will have been delivered.

If, however, even though a product is produced, there are many copies of it, each used by a different person, then the risk of inconsistency and variability creeps in. Something physical for which many copies are made can end up with not all of the copies being as close to the desired original specification, depending upon variations in the manufacturing processes.

If the deliverable is not nearly so tangible, then new challenges arise. Something like software can be capable of being replicated perfectly, if many copies are needed, but it is no longer the case that its quality can be determined just by examining it. Only when it is put to use will it become clear if it has the right level of quality.

This is part of the journey along the spectrum from tangible to intangible. If the deliverable is a service, then a different set of factors start to come into play. A service that is provided by an individual has a number of specific features. It is fleeting and you cannot bottle it and replay it; each time it is done, it will be done slightly differently. The same person delivering a given service may vary in terms of how they do so depending upon the way in which the recipient acts – so two different recipients of what should be the same service, provided by the same person, may well experience it very differently. The expectations of the recipient will have a significant bearing upon whether the service is deemed to have been of the right quality or not.

Complex projects can quite often deliver a mix of different types of deliverable, which when combined together result in the solution. The way in which the business will specify what it wants and then assess it will therefore reflect a combination of these different styles.

Another key dimension to quality is the concept of assumptions. Although it has been touched on before, in the case of quality it makes a significant difference. A given part of the business will have long-standing experience of how certain things are done and how a particular type of deliverable should look, work, be maintained and supported. To many in the business, these understandings are beyond obvious; they fall into the category of unspoken common sense. The business would have no reason to expect anyone to not know about this and to not realise that this is the obvious way that something should be created, used and looked after. Because it is so self-evident, the business tends to assume that everyone knows this already, and so it does not need to be stated. This is where a serious risk of mismatch in understanding can arise.

The business will work on the basis that the members of the project team are experts at what they do and therefore will naturally create solutions that work as the business would expect. Sometimes this may be satisfactory, but on other occasions the project team, although highly skilled at the technical elements of creating the desired deliverables, may not be particularly familiar with the ground rules of the business. A self-aware project team may question the business to get clarification and confirmation with regard to what is unsaid and unstated. This can unsettle the business as it exposes the lack of business familiarity of the project team. A wise business will find this reassuring as it indicates that the project has appreciated that there may be a blind spot that needs attention; however, this will not always be the case.

The corollary to this is that a thorough project will seek to understand, document and confirm a wide range of aspects of a solution that can strike the business as either unnecessarily detailed or wanting to tie it down and limit its flexibility. The business will tend to focus on the main way in which a solution will exist and be used, whilst a project will also want to consider all the other scenarios, some of which might be really quite unlikely, but that nonetheless still need to be analysed, defined and agreed. This focus on getting everything clear can prove frustrating to a business if it is particularly driven to get the main outcomes achieved as soon as possible. The appetite of the business to take on risk and accept that some aspects of the solution may not be fully clear and, if particular scenarios arise, may result in poor outcomes can vary considerably. Again, this, like the solution itself, is often tacit and is assumed by the business to be self-evident and something that the project should naturally be aware of already. Where there is a mismatch either way between the business' actual appetite for risk and the one that the project thinks that the business has, there is a real chance of ending up with a solution that is either under- or over-engineered.

An additional aspect that can be of interest to the business has a process dimension to it. It is not so much to do with the deliverable (i.e. the product quality or how the deliverable is used), the quality of the process required for turning the tangible deliverable into a solution, but rather focuses on the quality of the project experience for the business. Do the processes that the members of the project team follow, the way they work and the way in which they interact with the business give the business a feeling that it is dealing with a high-quality project team? This can be overlooked by the project, as the focus is on creating the deliverables, and the style of interaction with the business may not receive much attention. The project can be perfectly professional, but at the same time potentially rather insensitive to the business if it adopts a style that is at odds with the preferred culture and working methods of the business. Although not evident particularly at the end of the day, once the project has delivered, this aspect of quality can still have a significant impact on whether the business considers that the project was of the right quality or not.

The business viewpoint on quality can come from a different 'world' from that of project quality. Where a business provides a service, manufactures a product or operates in some way whereby many copies or instances of a product or service are provided to clients or customers, then a particular style of thinking about quality may already be present. This tends to relate to concepts focused on making sure that variation in outcome is minimised, such as Statistical Process Control, and that the efficiency of the operation is maximised using techniques such as Lean or Six Sigma. This area of quality tends to focus on repetitive processes with reasonable volumes, making sure that they are done well and that the outcome matches the specification time after time. However, the application of quality principles to projects is rather different due to the one-off nature of projects. This can lead to a different set of terminology and techniques being deployed, which can feel unfamiliar to the business and can cause frustration. The project approach to quality tends to focus very much on making sure that the requirements are fully understood, completely specified and then accurately turned into designs and then built. This usually involves a number of steps of specify, review, agree, freeze, build and test. To the business, this can feel very pernickety, tedious and slow. This can be exacerbated by the project approach to change management, whereby any adjustments that are requested by the business to an agreed baseline involve extensive impact analysis and tracing through how the changes will affect the rest of the solution, its cost to build and the timeline for its creation. If the business has a naturally tendency to spontaneity and creativity, this level of analysis can feel at the very least boring and can potentially crush its enthusiasm and commitment to the project.

The Project Perspective

The project perspective on quality will be different. The classic triangle of time-cost-quality means that if forced to meet a specific target in terms of time or cost, which are often closely linked, the project may find that it needs to compromise on quality. For seasoned project staff, this will not come as a surprise, but their approach to it may unsettle the business, as the need for these sorts of trade-offs may not be nearly so apparent to it.

The project team itself will not all think the same way. Most projects include an internal tension between those who focus very carefully on quality, particularly making sure that the processes that are traditionally associated with achieving high levels of quality are followed, and those who are more pragmatic and focused primarily on achieving the delivery goals even if the eventual solution has a number of rough edges that may need to be dealt with after the go-live point. Quite simply, quality will appeal to some team members but strike others as a bureaucratic slowdown.

If the project has a very strong quality process culture, this can actually reduce its responsiveness to the business. Some within the project team may feel that repeated uncertainty, mind-changing and vagueness by the business make it in some way a problem to be fought against rather than a partner with which to construct a solution. If these mismatches in approach persist over a period of time, the differing expectations of the two parties can drive a wedge between the two teams.

Bridging the Divide

To bridge the divide, a range of techniques can be considered. The aim here is to make sure that both parties are speaking the same language, so that differences in viewpoints, expectations and approaches are at least clear. This can enable the process of bringing the project and the business together to begin from a quality perspective.

The first area to consider is training. There is considerable merit in investing some time at the start of the project to make sure that each party understands what quality means to the other side, and how they go about achieving it. For the project, it is worthwhile explaining to the business what the quality methods are that the project intends to use, how the business can and should get involved in the processes, the benefits that the approach is intended to achieve and how that achievement will be greater if the business is also part of the process. This should be balanced by the business explaining what quality means to it, particularly in terms of maintaining operations and services, so that the two mindsets of the business and the project can explore common ground in their thinking and develop a way of working together.

If a solid foundation of understanding is established between the project and the business, then the joint team will be in a position to have a mature and considered discussion about the balances that are needed between time, cost and quality. It is important that this is not just done once near the start of the project. Circumstances will change, probably more than once, and pressures and problems will affect the nature and significance of particular requirements, the target timelines for the project, what is achievable in the light of problems encountered along the way, and the available budget and how it is being used up, which may be faster than originally planned. The balance between time, cost and quality therefore needs to be regularly sense-checked and periodically reset to match the evolving reality of the project.

The way that quality plays out in practice can have a number of interesting dimensions and it is well worth both the business and the project appreciating these from the start.

One classic consideration in terms of quality is that for the business, it is sometimes hard to specify in a document. The statement 'I'll know if it's good quality when I see it' tends to sum up this situation. For certain types of business, long, abstract paper-based specifications of what a solution should do, how it should look and what its features should be may not be particularly accessible and understandable. This can lead to frustration and push-back by the business if it feels overloaded with too much documentation to review. This is where a more practical approach by the project team can be beneficial. An approach that presents already-existing examples of what is to be constructed or created can provide a much more tangible and accessible reference point for the business to enable it to assess whether what is being proposed is actually what it wants. If real-world examples do not exist or cannot easily be obtained, then this approach can be extended to models and dry-run working sessions where analogous deliverables or practice process walkthroughs can again bring the abstract requirements on a written page into the tangible real world. This will make them more tractable from the point of view of the business, which can then determine what it really wants informed by practical experience and dry-runs to try out ideas and processes.

It is worth the business understanding the tensions that can exist within project teams. Project people often feel rewarded for delivering, not for following the rule book. In fact, delivery-focused project members, particularly highly confident ones, can be doubtful of the benefits of rule books full of processes and methods. As a result, the project may not be as disciplined and controlled as expected.

Projects that are undertaken by a separate supplier or in some cases by a unit within a business that has some sort of external accreditation, often against an international standard, will result in constraints being imposed on the way in which the project is run. It will be important to the organisation of which the project team is part that the certification is retained. This sort of accreditation is of benefit to the business as it should provide a degree of comfort that the project will be undertaken using good practice; however, on the flip-side this may limit the flexibility of the project team. The extent to which they are able to bend in order to respond to and accommodate the wishes of the business will be a function of how the standard that the members of the project team need to follow is being interpreted and how inherently flexible it is.

Sometimes the requirements of a certification can generate tensions both within the project and between the project and the business. This arises where there is a need for the project to ensure that its work generates evidence to enable certifications to be achieved or retained. This aspect of what needs to be produced is not always seen as the core focus for the delivery team and in particular, by the business, if it is not familiar with the demands of such certification schemes.

Separate but related to this is the audit and review regime that can be imposed upon a project. Depending upon the sector that the business solution will be delivered into and also the disciplines that the project team needs to follow, a potentially quite onerous and in some cases obligatory, audit and inspection regime may apply to the project. This can feel like a distraction to both the project team and the business. Ultimately there are normally good reasons for why such audit regimes exist, but the benefit they bring may not always be immediately obvious and can as a result get the quality angle within the project a bit of a bad reputation for excessive bureaucracy, risk aversion and focusing on what the business might feel is relatively unimportant minor details. In short, the auditors may not be welcome.

A related audit activity sometimes arises if the project appears to be running into trouble. This can result in a wish, often expressed by the sponsors, for an independent health check and assessment of the project. This is not so much an audit against a specific standard to determine compliance, but more of an informed review of the state of the project by a knowledgeable independent observer. These reviews quite often draw upon bodies of best practice to structure the checks that happen, and to formulate their report and recommendations. The intention is to determine whether the project is in as much trouble as some people may fear, or maybe less, or possibly more. In almost all cases, since these reviews cost money, they will only be undertaken if there is definitely some element of trouble. The recommendations will focus upon getting the project back on track, with proposed changes to how the project is being run.

Public and private views on an evaluation of a project may diverge in terms of what people want to put on the record. This type of review can be viewed as a negative imposition by the members of the project team, who will understandably be quite hostile to having their failings pointed out. Business team members may feel quite secure in their roles, but the project staff can feel vulnerable, since such reviews quite often recommend changes to project staffing, which basically puts members of the project team out of a job. Leaving a project in this way is also not good for career progression, so the project will tend to be motivated to minimise the scale of any problems that are uncovered. The business may be less resistant to the review, as they tend to believe that any problems reside with the project team, but they may be surprised if the review also highlights failings in the way the business has played its part in the project–business partnership. A good review mends fences and helps bring together warring factions, whereas a poor review can exacerbate troubles.

The set of structured guidance that the project follows, in order to enable it to achieve the desired level of quality, can be very useful, but it needs to be applied judiciously and with awareness and understanding. If such a support superstructure already exists, then it can be used to jump-start the project's approach to achieving and maintaining quality. In this case the way in which elements of the method are selected and used needs to be done with care and insight. The blanket application of every part of a method will tend to be an overload and end up being counter-productive.

However, a project that is operating in more of a vacuum, without such a readily accessible set of guidance, can be at a significant disadvantage. Most project professionals expect some sort of method to be available within the project organisation, and if it is not there, they will normally consider it worthwhile to invest some time in obtaining and/or creating the parts of such a method that the project needs. Doing this may slow down the start of the project and appear to the business as a waste of time, so the project needs to also invest some time in educating the business in why having such structured approaches to how it does its work will in the end make the rest of the project smoother, simpler and yield a higher-quality result. In some cases, projects are not in a position to wait for a set of guidance to be created around them and will often get started with off-the-shelf methods. This can be good, but again tailoring is vital. The unthinking application of a large rule book will simply over-complicate everything and end up being counter-productive.

One other aspect of methods is the extent to which they are supported by effective computer-based tools. This can be valuable, but the amount of time needed to get a tool up and running and adding value to a project will vary. Some tools can now be bought 'in the cloud' as services over the Internet, and so will be productive very quickly. However, the more complex and sophisticated the tool is, the more upfront effort and thinking is required to make sure that it is set up and configured in a way that will support rather than hinder the project process.

The effectiveness of methods to support how a project is run and how the business interacts with the project can vary over time. It is possible for methods to fall from regular use, if not actively supported and promoted, and as a result become shelf-ware. This will damage the credibility of the method, and it may start to become counter-productive. To deal with this, the organisation that the project team belongs to will need to reinvigorate the method, which is possible, with a refresh and rebranding. This can then lead to an increase in uptake, ideally through newly generated enthusiasm, which is preferable. Mandating is less effective, tends to work for short periods, is subject to grudging compliance and can then lead to the method being resented.

If these points are addressed, then a project and its business client can be brought together very effectively. Uniting around a common goal of making sure that the project delivers a solution and outcome that meets the understood and agreed quality requirements of all parties can give everyone a valuable unity of purpose.

Key Points

- Quality can be subjective, depending on the nature of what is being created by the project.

- The business will have long-standing experience of how certain things are done and how a particular type of deliverable should look, work, be maintained and supported.

- To many in the business, these understandings are beyond obvious; they fall into the category of unspoken common sense.

- The business will work on the basis that the members of the project team are experts at what they do, and therefore will naturally create solutions that work as the business would expect.

- The business will also be concerned with the quality of the project experience for the business.

- The business viewpoint on quality can relate to concepts focused on making sure that variation in outcome is minimised, such as Statistical Process Control, and that the efficiency of the operation is maximised using techniques such as Lean or Six Sigma.

- The project approach to quality tends to focus very much on making sure that the requirements are fully understood, completely specified and then accurately turned into designs and then built.

- A thorough project will seek to understand, document and confirm a wide range of aspects of a solution that can strike the business as either unnecessarily detailed or wanting to tie it down and limit its flexibility.

- If the project has a very strong quality process culture, this can actually reduce its responsiveness to the business.

- To bridge the divide, both parties need to understand the points made above and consider the following:

  - invest some time at the start of the project to make sure that each party understands what quality means to the other side, and how they go about achieving it;
  - engage in a mature and considered discussion about the balances that are needed between time, cost and quality;
  - this balance between time, cost and quality needs to be regularly sense-checked and periodically reset to match the evolving reality of the project;
  - gain a shared appreciation of the constraints imposed on the way in which the project is run by any external certifications;
  - discuss the benefits of inspections and audits, and how they can help the project rather than be seen as a bureaucratic distraction;
  - participate constructively in any project reviews – a good review mends fences and helps bring together warring factions, whereas a poor review can exacerbate troubles;
  - if guidance exists for project processes, discuss and agree how this will be followed;
  - if no guidance exists for project processes, the project needs to invest time in educating the business in why having such structured approaches will make the project smoother, simpler and yield a higher-quality result;
  - uniting around a common goal of making sure that the project delivers a solution and outcome that meets the understood and agreed quality requirements of all parties can give everyone a valuable unity of purpose.

Chapter 12
Planning and Execution

Planning and execution sit at the heart of a successful project. Execution consists of putting the plans into action and the subsequent tracking and reporting upon their achievement or otherwise. Comprehensive planning, proactive action taking, effective tracking and meaningful reporting will be a key determinant in the success or failure of a project. However, the two parties can often approach this with contrasting mindsets.

The Business Perspective

The first challenge people coming from a business viewpoint often face is that project planning is fundamentally different from regular business planning. Business planning follows a regular pattern and is intrinsically predictable. What is being planned may be different from year to year: do we grow, do we exit this market, do we sell our office and lease it back? However, irrespective of the content of the planning, the actual cycle of events tends to be very similar year in, year out. It is driven by a calendar dictated by the company year and is also influenced by the tax year, meaning that a number of months ahead, business people involved in planning can predict what they need to be doing, and if they have been doing it for a while, it will have become second nature to them.

The world of project planning is very different. The activity being planned is a one-off with a potentially uncertain outcome and the brigading together of a temporary workforce. Business planning by contrast is more focused on incremental adjustments to existing arrangements, potentially by redeploying existing resources, against a timeframe that may well be set by the annual cycle of organisational activity.

Business planning may not be so detailed. If there is an established pattern of how a particular part of an organisation runs, then additional tasks tend to be quite easily described and articulated, so planning may seem obvious and not really worth the paper that it is written on. However, for a project, especially for anything non-trivial with more than two parallel streams of activity, thorough planning becomes essential. In particular, good planning also forces out into the open the dependency sequence between tasks, which sometimes is not obvious.

The business may need coaching and occasionally training in project management techniques. A classic technique is the Gantt chart, which provides a very effective visual summary of a project. However, if the business is not familiar with this tool, then care needs to be taken on how it is introduced and used. Gantt charts can be very useful, but run the risk of being confusing, especially if they have more than 30 tasks, multiple levels of task grouping and need to be spread over more than one page of easy-to-read A4 paper.

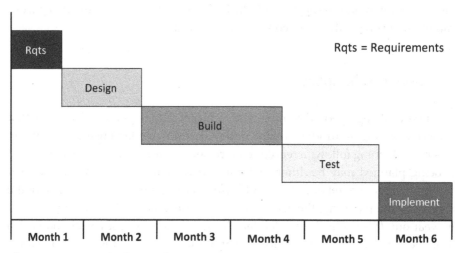

Figure 12.1   Basic Gantt chart

One element that the business will need to be an arbiter over is the go-live date. Even if a project can achieve a particular date, there may be other reasons that the business is aware of which constrain when go-live is possible. Here the project and the business may push in opposite directions. If there is an earlier go-live date that is potentially a bit risky and may not be achieved, the project could be keen to press on and have a go at trying to hit the date. Conversely, the business may not want to run the risk of failing to hit that date and would in fact prefer to settle on a go-live date that is later but more likely to be achievable.

It is also worth realising that project plans are very rarely right first time and are often not capable of being complete unless they undergo a number of cycles of discussion, review and revision. This iterative approach may prove frustrating to the business.

The Project Perspective

Effective planning lies at the core of a good project. Project people who have spent their working lives on projects will tend to treat this as second nature. They are likely to make assumptions about how up to speed other stakeholders are with the concepts, thought processes and practices of planning and execution.

Their approach to constructing the plan can be broken down into four main steps:

- Identify the deliverables that the project needs to produce, which will be a combination of final deliverables and interim deliverables that are the necessary staging posts and pre-cursors to the final deliverables.

- Define the tasks required to produce each of the deliverables, plus the tasks needed to coordinate the project as a whole. Place these tasks into an ideal timeline, so that if resources were not constrained, the project could be undertaken as quickly as would be possible.

- Identify the actual available resources and map them onto the tasks previously defined. It is quite possible that there will be some limitations to the resources that in practice the project can lay its hands upon. As a result, the ideal timeline will not be achievable and the project will actually need to take longer.

- This revised timeline may not be to the liking of the business, so at this point, the project will need to negotiate with the business in relation to this. It may be the case that resource constraints are a result of budget limitations and that if this is the case, the business may be persuaded to make available additional funds to enable further resources to be added to the project so that the timeline can end up being closer to the original ideal schedule.

Different project managers will approach this process in a way that suits them. The author's particular preference is for what can be described as an 'Outcome

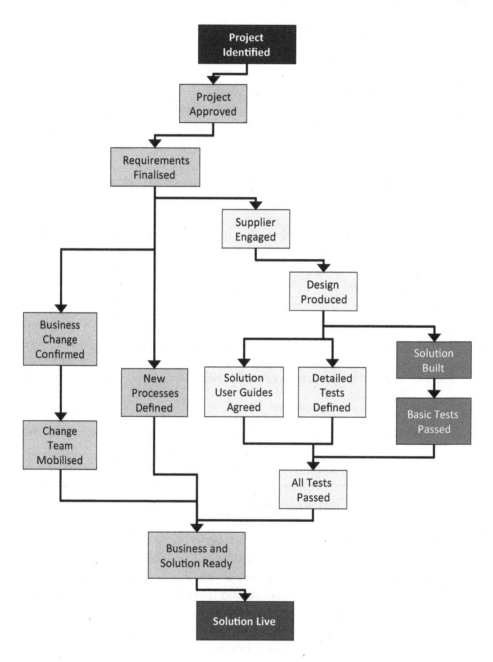

Figure 12.2   Outcome network

Network', which is similar to a Product Flow Diagram (Managing Successful Projects with PRINCE2™ 2009: 283).

A strong project manager realises that the plan is the servant of the project and not vice versa. This means that they may be quite pragmatic in terms of how strictly they follow it from day to day, but they will always keep in focus the ultimate goals of the project and ensure that all activities work consistently towards them.

Reporting styles vary, but effective reporting should always use the activities and the deliverables to form the basis for quantitative progress reporting. Put starkly, this is not a 'what I did on my holidays' narrative of whatever happened in the previous week – it is a very structured assessment of whether the expected activities happened as planned and whether the predicted status of the deliverables is as per the schedule for this point in the project.

Bridging the Divide

To bring together the differing perspectives of business and projects with regard to planning and execution, a range of techniques and areas merit attention.

RE-PLANNING

To the business, the activity of having to put the current plan on the shelf and undertake a re-plan can seem like an admission of having run into serious trouble. In fact, repeated re-planning does not indicate failure, but is perfectly normal. For the project, it illustrates healthy and necessary adaptation to evolving circumstances. No project can foresee everything at the start; if it tried to, it would never get started as it would be stuck in a paralysis of analysis. This positive view of re-planning can be taken for granted within the project team, but it needs to be explained to the business, preferably well ahead of it needing to be done.

JOINT PLANNING

Bringing together the business and the project teams into a joint planning session can be very effective. This approach is particularly good at identifying interdependencies, not just between 'internal' project deliverables within the project team, but also between the project, the shadow team and the wider environment. It can also give clarity to the right sequence in which to undertake tasks. For it to work well, an independent facilitator can often help, together with an approach that keeps the analysis at the right level. Spending all the time getting the first 25 per cent of the project planned perfectly in great detail is actually less useful than having the full end-to-end lifecycle roughed out so that everyone can see and agree on the big picture.

RESOURCE CONSTRAINTS

One aspect of planning that tends to be second nature for the project team is the knowledge, often gained via painful experience, that doubling the resources will not necessarily halve the project's duration. This is not always the case with a day-to-day business process, where if you double the number of staff doing a particular task, provided you are not physically resource-constrained, you may be able to halve the time taken. It will depend upon the divisibility and parallel working features of the task. A simple process that is quick to teach and simple to split into smaller tasks, which can be done at the same time by different people, is amenable to resource step-up. A project is often knowledge work that cannot be easily divided, in addition to which the extra resources (even if they could be delivered to order) would probably need significant induction into the project and would then need to regularly communicate with other project team members. An additional overhead of more coordination would also be required.

Number of People	Number of Communications Routes	Communications Network
2	1	
3	3	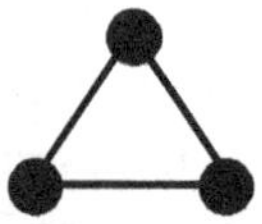
4	6	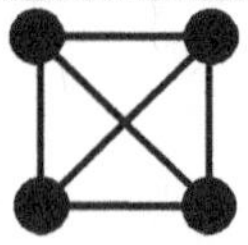
5	10	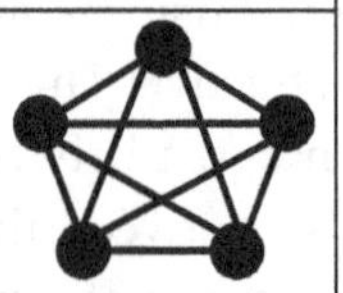

Figure 12.3   Increasing complexity of communications as team size grows

Each additional person added into a team whose members need to regularly interact with each other increases the number of communication links required.

Taking all of this together, doubling the project workforce is very unlikely to halve the duration, and in fact there will come a point when adding an additional person will come with so many overheads that it will not shorten the project at all. Doing this during the planning phase is one thing, but trying to ramp-up resources once the project has run into difficulties is much harder. In short, throwing extra resources at later phases, especially if this is done in catch-up mode, may not actually speed up the project at all, just cost it more money and get it into a worse hole in terms of the cost element of the time-cost-quality balance.

CONTINGENCY SQUEEZING

Although very tempting and an easy target, squeezing contingency out of a schedule is often unwise. The business can feel that the project is giving itself a get-out clause, letting itself off the hook, if it builds in a buffer of time or resources that appears not to be needed. The pressure coming from multiple reviews of an evolving budget often pares away at the contingency, putting the project into a position whereby, if something takes an unexpected turn, there is no spare time, money or resources to get it back into line. It can be quite a difficult thing for the project to fight for and to retain its contingency, especially since this is likely to need to happen right at the start of the project, possibly before strong and trusting working relationships have been established between the project team and the business team. Nonetheless, it is very wise to agree to retain some contingency, otherwise recovery, should any problems arise, can be more difficult and costly than it otherwise would have been.

Some projects make use of a starting point that can end up being a bottleneck. If the resources in the project organisation are constrained and it is using an already-existing technical solution to form part of its deliverables, then problems can ensue. In particular, the same product, differently configured and extended for multiple clients, can put clients in a queue for upgrades due to resources or dependencies. This can delay a particular project unexpectedly and it might find that it needs to compete for its place in the queue.

There are times when projects actually sit together with other projects in a wider construct. They are brought together either because they are all being provided for the same client, because they are being performed by the same organisation or because they share some common technology or approach that makes it sensible to group them together. This situation – where projects are part of programmes and portfolios – can be complex and it is not always clear to the business how they all fit together. The consequences that can follow from this are mixed; some skills and functions that a solo project would not be able to afford can be shared across a programme or portfolio. However, the fitting together of all the projects can lead to a variety of types of competition for resources, whether physical, informational and human. Achieving the optimum outcome for an overall programme of interlinked projects may not be so beneficial for an individual project if it has to compromise on where it comes in the planned sequence, and if it has dependencies on other projects in the programme that run into trouble and fail to provide expected inputs to the project at the time and date originally agreed.

Classic examples of the sort of complex programme that a project can end up being part of include business units being set up from scratch or maybe being moved into a new organisation via a merger. These will often require many interlinked projects to be undertaken all at the same time.

In relation to the changes resulting from mergers and reorganisations, when an organisation is going through such a process, it can have an impact on the project world. In particular, acquisitions and disposals can themselves cut across projects that are ongoing, disrupting previously set timelines. This sort of change is by its nature undertaken with a degree of confidentiality which means that it may only become common knowledge quite late. As a result, a project may be well underway before it is realised that it will be unavoidably affected and will need to be re-planned and adjusted to reflect the changed circumstances. In addition, such acquisitions and disposals can result in key members of a project or shadow project team being distracted or even reallocated away from the project, compounding the problems faced by the project. This is often not predictable and is to a large extent unavoidable; the main way to deal with it is to be aware that in some situations this might happen and have contingency plans in place.

METHODS

The approach taken by the project as to how it goes about planning and executing its work can be significantly enhanced where it makes use of established good practices. The extent to which such a supporting method is in place can vary quite considerably. Some organisations will have nothing and each project will have to be self-supporting. Some businesses may have fragmented sets of procedures which could benefit from being brought together into unified project management systems, but nonetheless provide some level of support. Others may have a highly developed, extensive and mature set of well-defined project working practices, which if used appropriately can give the project a springboard into its planning, tracking and reporting.

Care needs to be taken to use such sets of procedures selectively, as their wholesale application without the use of balancing common sense judgement can lead to a project being swamped in bureaucracy and this sort of approach gaining a bad press with the business team. It is also vital that the members of the business team are introduced to the method so that they understand what it is, why it is followed, what benefits using it brings and what their role is in making the approach a success.

Change is a constant, particularly in a project delivery organisation. Turnover in staff means that new people in an organisation may well not be aware of the standard methods and approaches for project management. This can lead to a project not using the best practice approaches that the organisation already knows. Care therefore needs to be taken in terms of induction at two levels, once when joining the organisation and also when joining a particular project team, in case the first induction did not happen properly or was not effective.

Detail matters and this is where methods can help. Projects rarely go back and document things after a particular phase has passed. So if the business wants something in writing, it needs to make sure that it is done 'in-line' whilst that phase is still happening. The challenge arises, however, because the business may not always be clear what it wants and needs documented. In addition, it may assume that a project will naturally document all that is required, when in fact this activity has fallen by the wayside. The use of structured methods, and particularly checklists that can form the basis for reviews, can help to bring such situations out into the light and enable areas that might otherwise get missed to be captured whilst the information is still fresh in everyone's minds.

ALTERNATIVE PERSPECTIVES

Bringing the business and the project together on a regular basis to discuss how the other side sees things can be illuminating and helpful. A classic example is where a series of small projects undertaken by a large project-based organisation can become quite slow and bureaucratic. With a set of well-defined steps followed a little too mechanically, the result can be that the project does not appear to be very responsive to the business. This is where dialogue can help.

Such practices can also help to set the scene and facilitate mature conversations between the business and project that enable 'unaskable' questions to be raised and considered. In particular, one of the most difficult questions relates to the concept of an immovable end date, in short: 'Is it really fixed?' The answer might be yes, it might be no – this is actually less important than having the maturity of business-project relationship to be able to consider asking this question. It is good to be able to do so and to then have a civilised fact-based conversation about it so that a valid and reasoned decision can be reached about how much flexibility there really is in the end date.

LOGISTICS

The logistical aspects of a project can seem relatively insignificant when compared to more sophisticated technical challenges. As it happens, they can in fact make or break a project, even a well-planned one.

Any project involving the delivery of physical items to a range of geographical locations can be subject to logistical problems that may seem relatively trivial, such as materials or people not arriving on time at the right location. However, this can be compounded by disruptions due to weather and illness. The challenge here is that a project in an office is less vulnerable to missing a person or equipment item, but at a remote location, the absence may knock back a schedule by a day or two. If this happens a number of times or at a variety of locations, then over time and, faced with a tight schedule, the individual delays soon add up to something that is significant enough to result in a non-trivial delay to the project. From a business team perspective, this sensitivity to such problems may not be obvious, and so it is worth including in the joint-teaming induction activities when planning is first undertaken. It also reinforces the benefits of including enough contingency to cover such unforeseen events.

The logistical aspects of working locations can have positive benefits for a project. Project teams that are set up away from home (on or near a client site) and therefore stay away from home during the week (quite often all in the same hotel) can bond quickly and effectively, and as a result tend to have a higher productivity level. The project can spill over into evenings, with a project team eating together and continuing to discuss the project. Provided that some allowance is made to achieve a modicum of work-life balance, this can lead to a 'hot-house' approach that generates a step-change in team effectiveness and efficiency.

A related aspect can be where a project is multi-site based across different time zones. This can also include a situation where the business is located in a different time zone from the project team. For a multi-zone project team, the project could be designed to 'follow the sun' and have work started by one team handed across to the next team at the first team's end of day, with the second team picking up and continuing the work during the first team's night. This will only really work for intangible deliverables such as documents and software. Care also needs to be taken to establish good working relationships between the teams, maybe co-locating them at the start of the project.

A more complex variant can involve different activities being sequenced in such a way that again they can be handed around the world. Challenges can exist in regulating and managing such arrangements, and rectifying problems can take longer if one team has to wait for the other team to become available again, with one or both teams coming in early and/or staying late to achieve a more complete discussion and resolution of any issues. Where the business and project are time-zone separated, the productivity gains may need to be balanced against the reduced levels of effective communication and interaction. This is where modern technology – in the form of video conferencing, phone and web conferencing – becomes essential to maintaining a strong partnership across such geographical distances. Reflecting this in the planning can be tricky. Should higher productivity be assumed, or might the barriers to communications slow things down and offset any potential benefits? This may need to be determined on a case-by-case basis.

FITTING IT ALL TOGETHER

A project consists of subsets of related tasks that can be relatively self-contained and potentially delivered by independent groups within the overall project team. However, making sure that all these elements fit together is important to realising the goals of the project.

It is worth getting maximum clarity about all the dependencies that these teams will have upon each other. Assumptions relating to these, particularly tacit assumptions, and even just lack of awareness that the dependency exists are very good at tripping up a project. Diagrammatic representations of dependencies can make it clearer how a project needs to fit together and interact with other projects and external activities. Sharing these across the team and with the business can give everyone the same understanding of the challenges faced by the project and the business.

The human dynamic can overlay a complication onto the puzzle of getting the teams to work together for the greater good of the project. Within a large, stressed and resource-limited project, particular teams can end up competing with each other for resources, and the team that is best at internal politics (or has the most power) will gain the resources and deliver their segment of the project, but potentially at the expense of other teams and segments, which in the big picture might have been more important.

FINAL THOUGHT ON PLANNING

Always expect the unexpected. Do not assume that because one part of a project is going to be delivered that an element of it might not be missing at a crucial moment, causing a critical delay or failure. It may not sound appealing to the business and may need to be introduced as a concept gradually, but the approach to project planning and execution that yields fewest surprises and least stress is to be optimistic and hope for the best, but at the same time to be realistic and plan for the worst.

Key Points

- Business planning follows a regular pattern and is intrinsically predictable.

- Business planning is more focused on incremental adjustments to existing arrangements set by the annual cycle of organisational activity.

- Even if a project can achieve a particular date, there may be other reasons that the business is aware of which constrain when go-live is possible.

- The world of project planning is very different; the activity being planned is a one-off with a potentially uncertain outcome and the brigading together of a temporary workforce.

- Good planning forces out into the open the dependency sequence between tasks, which sometimes is not obvious.

- Constructing the plan will divide into four main steps:

  - identify the deliverables that the project needs to produce;
  - define the tasks required to produce each of the deliverables, plus the tasks needed to coordinate the project as a whole;

- identify the actual available resources and map them onto the tasks previously defined;
- this revised timeline may not be to the liking of the business, so at this point the project will need to iteratively refine the plan by negotiating with the business.

- Project plans are very rarely right first time and are often not capable of being complete unless they undergo a number of cycles of discussion, review and revision.

- To bridge the divide, both parties need to understand the points made above and consider the following:

  - a shared education process about the benefits of regular re-planning;
  - bring together the business and the project teams into a joint planning session;
  - make sure that all parties understand that doubling the project resources will not necessarily halve the duration of project;
  - reach an appreciation that squeezing contingency out of a schedule is often unwise;
  - be clear on the relationship between an individual project and the context of a larger more complex programme of which it may be part;
  - identify how best to make use of predefined methods that may be available;
  - bring the business and the project together on a regular basis to discuss how the other side sees things can be illuminating and helpful;
  - deliberately consider and analyse the importance of logistics to the project, and what impact logistical problems might have;
  - obtain maximum clarity about all the dependencies that individual teams will have upon each other;
  - be optimistic and hope for the best, but at the same time be realistic and plan for the worst.

Chapter 13

HR

Already in this book, the importance of the human dimension to project management has been emphasised. It is now time to turn the focus more directly on this area. HR (Human Resources) is a classic 'business as usual' discipline, so let us start by looking at this more closely.

The Business Perspective

The nature of a business, providing a product or service on an ongoing basis, means that the organisational structure for 'business as usual' functions tends have a different flavour from that of a project.

The organisation chart is often fixed and stable for a business cycle (quite often a financial year). Restructures might be regular, but will also be predictable, in terms of their timing, and foreseeable, with regard to who might be due for a promotion. Significantly, post-holders tend to have career paths laid out for them that often involve progressing up a silo of skill, at least until they reach a senior management level. This means that there is a degree of predictability about the business and how it manages, organises and motivates its people. To people on a project team, which is constantly changing, this may feel too predictable and even boring.

AN ANALOGY FOR THINKING ABOUT ORGANISATIONAL STRUCTURES

An analogy can sometimes help with understanding certain ideas. The author has a particular preference for thinking about organisational structures in terms of life-rafts floating on the sea. This may sound a little odd, but stay with it, as it does actually bring out some valuable perspectives. Imagine a ship that has sunk: all the people who were on board are safe and they are all now in life-rafts. Something of a pecking order applies in that the more senior individuals each have their own life-raft, whilst groups of the more junior ones have to share. If a spotter plane, searching for them before the rescue helicopter or boat arrives, were to look down on the flotilla from above, it would see the rafts spread out across the sea. Now stretching the point slightly, the rafts could be laid out in such a structure, east–west and north–south, so as to correspond to an organisation chart (this wouldn't help them be rescued, but it does help the analogy). The diagram below shows this. Notice how the rafts are 'tied together' with 'rope'.

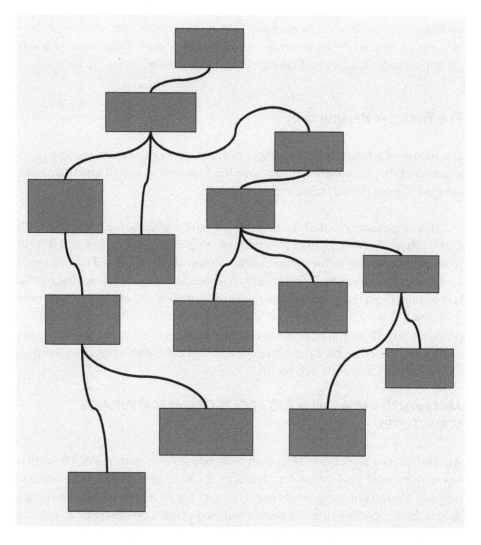

Figure 13.1   Organisational structure analogy

The situation in which the rafts find themselves enables us to highlight a number of features for an organisation's structure.

The sea is never completely calm. This means that the rafts are bobbing up and down, but are also drifting nearer and further away from each other. With no active intervention from anyone, the organisation can in effect subtly reconfigure itself with groupings of certain people and teams getting nearer or further away from each other.

If the relatively calm waters turn into something more choppy, strain may be put on the ropes linking the rafts and they can be stretched to breaking point. A raft may then be floating free and not attached to the organisation; it floats past another raft and someone there could throw it a line and reel it in. It would then be re-attached to the organisation, but in a different location. Some less lucky rafts might just float off into open ocean, never to be seen again. This is what a re-organisation can feel like.

In short, an organisation is never 100 per cent stable and fixed; it is always experiencing minor perturbations, but from time to time, often quite unpredictably, a storm can blow up and a major re-organisation can completely reconfigure the structure.

Interesting unintended consequences can flow from such situations. A storm might tip some people off their rafts and then sink the raft. These people no longer have a position in the organisation. They could swim to another raft and then, depending upon their inclination and level of stress, a dispute could break out with the occupant of that raft, and following a fight, one or other would end up in the sea, with the victor on the raft as the person who has survived the re-organisation.

Even when there is not a storm raging, more ambitious people might take a risk and swim to a new raft in order to attempt to get a better position. The level of risk is sometimes hard to determine, as the raft they jumped off might not still be there if they need to get back to it. The water might also contain sharks, so such attempts are often made only by the braver members of an organisational structure.

The rafts themselves may not be fully watertight. In other words, in order to stay afloat, the occupants need to be bailing water out continuously. This is analogous to the 'day job', which can quite often involve rather a lot of effort just to maintain one's position in the organisation without responding to change or attempting advancement.

A final thought is that as the helicopter approaches to rescue the occupants of the rafts, it has a good aerial view of the whole constellation of positions. This may not necessarily be the case for the people on the rafts. With the sea rising and falling, they will probably only be able to see the rafts next to them and have little if any contact with the rafts two or three positions away. This is very analogous to individuals being able to deal with their direct subordinates and direct superiors, but not having much contact higher or lower along the chain of command, and similarly working in silos and not having much read-across to people in other remote teams.

The arrival of a project can be akin to a flotilla of speedboats arriving into this mix. Some of the people on the rafts stop bailing out water to help with the project, their rafts may start to sink and their colleagues will start to resent them getting involved in the project and for not pulling their weight in their day job. Meanwhile, the members of the project team in their speedboats are linked far less tightly together, they move rapidly, they might slice through an organisational linkage without realising and the wash from one of their boats might swamp a raft. They will only be around for a short time and will then roar off into the distance, leaving a reconfigured and potentially rather overwhelmed organisational structure.

This example may have helped, if it did that's good, if not, feel free to leave it aside. Let us turn to other considerations.

OTHER CONSIDERATIONS

There tend to be a number of dimensions to the HR view of the world. First and foremost, everyone in the business is a person. Sometimes this means they are viewed as individuals and sometimes as units of resource to undertake work, but in either case always as people entitled to respect and fairness in how they are treated. In addition, an HR function will take a people-centric view of the organisation, using this as the lens through which it observes the organisation, rather than a view coloured by process, finance or technology.

The intersection between the business and the project is certainly in part mediated by the HR function. It is very likely to have a role to play in a project both in terms of staffing-up an in-house project team and also in relation to helping to make the organisational changes that a project might deliver happen.

One of the challenges that HR can face in trying to help get these changes to be realised is the role of business incentives. Staff in the 'business as usual' part of the organisation tend to be aligned to delivering the day job, not to project deliverables or the timelines with which they need to be produced. These patterns of motivation and reward will have been established over long periods of corporate history and the mindset of a time-bound quick-moving project can feel quite alien. In addition, the organisational structure which may (or may not) be aligned to business processes is most unlikely to be a good fit with project processes.

The transition into the project world for business staff is therefore quite often rather painful. Business people can be dropped into the deep end of a project without enough background briefing, leaving them 'all at sea'.

In addition, the business people who become part of the shadow team are likely to become overloaded as more often than not, their day job is squashed into three-quarters of their time and a quarter of their week is allocated to supporting the project. Day-job responsibilities do not shrink, merely the time available to do them, and when combined with project responsibilities that tend to be very variable in size and timing (in short, lumpy and unpredictable) can yield a significant amount of overload and resultant grief. Conflicting priorities and loyalties can lead to missed deadlines, affecting both the business and the project, and causing significant stress for the individuals concerned. In addition, where people from the business have been involved in previous projects, this may well have been their experience. As a result, their perceptions of the next project can be negatively affected by these earlier bad experiences.

These problems can be compounded if, late in the day, it is realised that the person from the business needs to be dedicated full time to the project. There may be a gap before a replacement to backfill their old business role can be found and trained in the business role. This will impact the business and the project can be perceived as having caused damage to the day-to-day business as a result of its demands for staff to be released from the business to work on the project.

The Project Perspective

The project view of the human dimension to projects is often quite different. The key feature of a project is that it is forever fluid, evolving and never the same in terms of structure and post-holders for more than a couple of weeks. This change is relentless, as the temporary organisation is created, adjusted, needs to adapt to change, evolves and re-forms due to the project moving through its lifecycle, before finally, after many transformations, winding down and disbanding, leaving only an empty office – and hopefully a solution owned and used by a satisfied business.

People who work in the project world have a different style of career path from 'business as usual' staff. The project person may specialise in a particular part of a project lifecycle (e.g. design or testing), but even so, they rarely have two days that are the same. A stint of a few months will itself have a lifecycle of stages and steps. Some other project people will stay with a project from start to finish, particularly those undertaking managerial or support roles. In all cases, once the project has finished, they are very likely to be gone, particularly if they are external to the business. This 'bell curve' of staffing is viewed as quite normal by experienced project people, who are used to the overlapping nature of multiple projects happening at the same time, with more senior staff staying from start to finish, and a cohort of more junior resources arriving a little later and leaving a little earlier. They are also familiar with the challenges of knowledge transfer both at the onboarding and also the exit points.

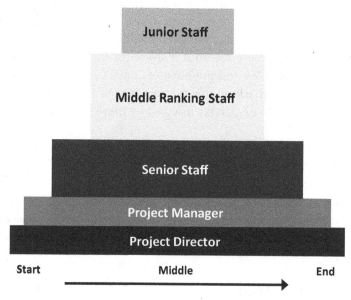

Figure 13.2   Staff seniority levels during the project lifecycle

Even if they are internal, their careers tend to involve frequent moves within and between project-shaped organisations, so that their next project will already attract their attention and focus, meaning that the just completed project will find it very hard to get access to the people who have recently rolled off.

This dynamic environment has implications for the business. In particular, the cycle time required for support functions to provide services to the project, notably for the hiring-in of project resources, can be much shorter than for appointing a business resource. A project might be spinning its wheels, burning money whilst waiting for the right crucial resource or, equally problematically, might start off without the right skill-set in place and then need to do re-work to correct mistakes. Thus, the timeline for recruitment is shorter than for business as usual.

Project people can have careers inside an organisation that has a projects section, so they maintain a bit of a career path where the projects section is part of the overall business (classically in the form of an in-house IT department). Alternatively, they may work for a company that provides project style services to other organisations, in which case each project will be for a different client, but the project person does have a career within the project services organisation. Finally, they may be freelance and arrange their own projects without being part of a wider organisation. All of these flavours of career path have one thing in common, in that to grow and challenge themselves, project people often aim for a bigger assignment and more responsibility on each successive project. Some consultancy organisations even deliberately push their staff into ever more stretching role, so as to weed out the weaker staff and then promote the stronger ones. As a result, within an individual project, the new project role-holders are often being stretched in their new roles as part of their career development. There can be a dynamic tension here, as the new challenge may be very good for the project team member, provided it gives them the right amount of stretch. However, having someone who appears to be ever so slightly out of their depth, sometimes 'drowning rather than waving', is not necessarily re-assuring for the business. Although a similar pattern of promotion into new more stretching roles can apply within the business, its more stable and hierarchical structure and can provide a better support mechanism to enable the newly promoted person to get to grips with their role. Project teams being assembled often from people who have not worked together before, and faced with tight deadlines right from the start, are less likely to have the support structures together with the time and space needed to support a newly promoted project person to learn by trial and error on the job.

One thing that can surprise the business is the style and approach that project people may use. They often consider that they are going to be judged on getting the project done, maybe at the expense of relationships and stepping on a few toes. It is possible that they may even have been engaged by some part of the business with this in mind. Since they will not be around after the project, ending up with bad relationships with others is less of a problem. What matters to the project professional will be: did they deliver? There will be a presumption in their mind that an on-time, to-quality and within-budget delivery will demonstrate their capability and lead to a satisfied business client. If noses were put out of joint in the process, then so be it. As a result, the type of reference that the business may give to the project person may come as a surprise, since sometimes it is the rough edges that linger in the corporate memory after the delight at the solution has faded.

Although, in general, they are well adapted to stress and are comfortable with it, seasoned project people can still be put under considerable pressure from time to time. Being in a project team can be quite painful if the individual is forever going from one stressful late-running project to another. Even within the same project, the level of turbulence can make an impact. Every few weeks things are different – a new phase, new tasks. Sometimes a resource can have roles in multiple projects that are being done in parallel and some team members may be spread across projects, which can lead to difficulties in terms of task and resource balancing. If problems arise in relation to the quality of deliverables, then stress will definitely ensue. Even just repeating work due to changes to the specification can be demoralising for the project team.

So we are faced with two sets of stressed people who may not fully understand each other. What can be done to bring them together?

Bridging the Divide

The challenge here goes to the heart of the dilemma. The project world and the business world can exist as two cultures and two camps, with two sets of loyalties. The best way to overcome this is with a set of joint activities.

JOINT WORKING

Co-locating business and project staff and, where possible, creating mixed teams so that barriers do not necessarily evolve in the first place is a useful strategy. This working together can lead to a number of the actions described below happening as a byproduct, without the need for deliberate intervention.

However, depending upon time pressures, it may be wise to deliberately choose to undertake some of the actions so that there is a guarantee that they will happen rather than that they may arise in a haphazard pattern by luck.

SHADOWING

If schedules will permit it, it can be useful for members of the business to spend a few days shadowing someone in the project and then vice versa. The level of understanding achieved will vary and depend upon how committed the individuals are to sharing their experience and approaches, how open-minded the person doing the shadowing is, and the patience of the person being shadowed. The outcome is not always certain and, in particular, not controllable. If the relationship gets off to a poor start, there is a small risk that it might do more harm than good. But this risk is probably worth taking, especially if a number of shadowing actions are taking place at the same time. The effort involved in terms of 'down time' for the person doing the shadowing can feel like a loss in efficiency; however, the payback should be that many later stages will run more smoothly and any 'lost time' will be more than regained by a more productive and harmonious working partnership for the rest of the project.

INDUCTION

Where a project and a business have induction programmes for their respective staff, it can be valuable to cross-fertilise the teams by sending business people on the project induction course and vice versa. Although this does not necessarily give them the first-hand experience that shadowing would, it does provide a good, carefully thought-through structured introduction to the other part of the equation and sets the scene for better mutual comprehension.

AWARENESS

There are two elements to awareness: the direct element, which focuses on making each team aware of the concerns and viewpoints of the other team; and the meta element, which involves alerting all the participants to the possibility that there may already be a gap there or that one is at risk of evolving. If this is pointed out, then a conscious attempt can be made to minimise it and a deliberate message will go out that the senior management overseeing the project want to make sure that it functions as a single effective and cohesive unit, and is not riven by disputes.

TRAINING

The classic and in some ways most obvious way to bring the two parties together is training. There are three aspects to a suitable curriculum:

- The first area would relate to an overview and introduction to project management itself. This book would be capable of forming a sensible basis for such an overview.

- The second area would involve delving deeper into the business role and perspective, covering what the business participants would need to do at each phase of a project and what their areas of focus and concern are likely to be.

- The third area would be a complementary exploration, at the same level of depth, of the project team activity and perspective. It would be crucial that all participants attended the whole course so that they got to understand the other party's viewpoint and also see their reactions to the explanations of their own viewpoint.

Given the levels of staff movement within a project, a regular re-run of the course would be vital. The course needs to be well developed and concise so that it does not take the team away from the project and day jobs for longer than is necessary. There is also a side benefit in that by putting all the project and business team members together on a course at the start of the project process, barriers between them start to be broken down and a combined team spirit can start to develop. To do this, care needs to be taken with some of the smaller details, for instance, seating plans should be developed so that the two groups do not sit in separate huddles, but instead are seated next to each other in an alternating 'business-project-business-project' fashion. If the sessions cover more than half a day, then each new half-day should have a different seating plan, again to force people to sit next to people who they otherwise would not have met or know.

MINIMISING GEOGRAPHICAL BOUNDARIES

Even if it is not possible to co-locate all of the team, it is still well worth trying to minimise geographical separation. Put simply, the nearer the better: the same floor is best, adjacent floors (that can be reached via stairs rather than lift) is next best, then further apart in the same building. These are all good because they do not involve putting on a coat and battling with the weather to reach the other half of the team. Anything more than this will start to induce a degree of inertia, a temptation to email or phone rather than to get together physically. Next best would be adjacent builds in the same development, street or campus, then getting worse, the same town, the same motorway corridor, the same time zone, the same country and the same continent. As we progress down the list, the barriers get bigger and will take more deliberate effort to overcome. This is still well worth it, but wherever there is a choice of locations, go for the one that gives the most real interaction.

If separation is inevitable, it can be helpful in the early days to make special short-term efforts to co-locate in the early weeks. Once face-to-face relationships have been established, the use of various technology options to shrink distances (e.g. video conferencing) can be far more effective than if done 'from cold' without having some shared bonding first.

SHARED INCENTIVES

Incentives often drive behaviour. These always exist and will probably have arisen over time, maybe by design, possibly just by evolution, and within both the business and project teams. However, they may not be particularly well suited to making the project a success. It very much depends upon what staff feel they are being rewarded for doing and also what they need to avoid doing so as not to suffer punishment. 'Business as usual' cultures and project cultures will tend to have different sets of incentives, and these can conflict. The members of the business team may prioritise getting the day job done and put project tasks to the end of their to-do lists, while the members of the project team may be so driven to hit an end date that they may end up viewing the business as an inconvenience to be ignored or worked around. It is only by taking a step back and designing a coherent and cohesive set of norms and reward structures that cover both the business and the project that progress will be maximised. These incentives need to be mutually reinforcing, so that all parties are encouraged to work in a way that helps the other party to succeed as well, and is focused on the overall objective of achieving not just an on-time delivery, but also a successful outcome for the business. This may sound like a luxury, but there is always a culture in all organisations – it is just a case of whether it has arisen by accident or whether it has been deliberately designed and effectively rolled out. To achieve this, ongoing active support will be needed – a one-off event will not be enough to make such cultural changes stick, so it needs to be an area of continual focus.

COMBINED SOCIALISING

Socialising together may not seem like an obvious way to increase professional understanding, but meeting away from a work environment and seeing each other as real people rather than 'the business' or 'the project' can help develop much more trusting and effective working relationships.

There are a number of human aspects that can manifest themselves in either or both of the business and the project teams. They are worth taking into account because they can affect joint working more than might be expected.

It is quite possible that project teams may be split between managers who are less technical and team members with deep technical knowledge. To the business, this split may not be so obvious. What the business will then not realise is that there can be real communication problems within the project team between these two groups. More often than not, it will be the managerial levels of the project team that interact with the business, and the business may presume that the project staff will have all aspects of the project at their fingertips. If the two groups within the project are not working well together, then this potential disharmony will be echoed and possibly magnified between the project overall and the business.

There are related issues in multi-style project teams. Projects that bring together mixed-skill teams from very different sectors – for instance, business strategy and on-the-ground operations – can run into real difficulties in forming a cohesive team. People's natural working styles, which have been built up over time and are perfectly normal within their specialism, will tend to clash; for instance, do we plan first then take action or alternatively get stuck in and assess if it is right as we go?

Extending further this consideration of the mixed project team, where there are supplier consortia, it is possible that internal tensions can arise that will divert the project from focusing on the delivery to the business. Multi-party consortia all need their own internal agreements, often legal contracts. Each separate organisation will also have its own style. This means that building a cohesive, coherent and efficient unified project team can be quite an undertaking.

Where projects are provided by project delivery organisations, which specialise in projects, the history of the organisation can have a significant bearing. It is quite common for such a project delivery organisation to be built by a series of takeovers or acquisitions. Changing the name plate on the front door and the logo on the website can be quick and easy; however, the other aspects of internal integration will take a lot longer. As a result, the project delivery organisation may not be as seamless on the inside as it likes to appear to a client. The internal structures, potential discomfort felt by staff as a result of the changes and possible poor communications, can all hamper its ability to act as a cohesive whole in support of its projects. Although on the face of it, this may be of no concern to the client business, which simply expects the project to deliver, an appreciation of its supplier's internal structures and politics will help the business to be at the very least forearmed and certainly less surprised if the project team does not always appear as unified as might be expected.

Projects are classic examples of rapidly growing organisations, even if they are relatively short-lived. The underlying precepts still apply, however. Rapidly growing organisations need to re-learn their processes regularly, particularly as new people arrive and new structures are established. Project working practices can be picked up by osmosis, but this is one of the less efficient ways to pass on such arrangements. Indeed, each time the rules are handed across informally, they are likely to get subtly misinterpreted and potentially evolve into something that was not intended. At the very least, consistency of execution is likely to be lost. In addition, rapidly growing organisations are not always the best at communicating their vision and keeping everyone up to speed on where they are going. In particular, once projects grow beyond a particular size, it is hard for all the members to know everything about what else is going on, and as a result which key items need to be shared. Growth is both demanding and exhilarating, leaving very little discretionary time available. As such, a growing team can accidentally become quite 'siloed' and people can assume that everyone knows what is going on, what the goals and plans are, when, in fact, if they are new or in a remote location, they quite possiblly do not. Active steps need to be taken to regularly check for this and to take action to overcome it whenever there appears to be a risk that a silo culture is developing.

The business side of the undertaking can also be affected by its multi-unit structure. It is quite likely that multi-division organisations will have different local practices which will affect how different parts of the business interact with the same project. Although the project may assume all parts of business will be on the same page, this will not always be the case.

Taking this further, where an organisation needs to change and a number of departments will be involved, each tends to see the change through the lens of its own specialism. This will tend to give rise to different sets of assumptions about what is normal, obvious and easy, and also what is more difficult. This can impact the overall project where it needs all of these different business teams to contribute to making a change happen.

Both the project and the business need to guard against knowledge loss. This can arise for a number of reasons. For the business, if a project involves relocations, then quite often staff can be lost to the business. One prudent rule of thumb that can be applied to a relocation is that a third of staff will not move and in effect leave the business at the time of relocation, while another third will move but very much on the basis of giving it a try and then may drift away within a year or so. This means that only the final third moves and stays. This is not a scientific finding, but rather an observation by the author based on witnessing a number of these situations over the years. The result is that within a couple of years following a relocation, it is possible that two-thirds of an organisation's staff may no longer be around and hence there is a real risk that some of the key knowledge they held may be lost. Whether this is the exact percentage in any given situation is not the critical point here. What is significant is that it would be wise to plan for a worst-case outcome where a sizeable proportion of staff were no longer in place a year after a relocation, and to take steps to ensure that all relevant knowledge is retained, and not lost, as a result of departures on such a scale.

Another aspect of restructuring is that when a business is re-organised, skills, expertise and organisational structures that support project management can be inadvertently lost, setting back the ability of the organisation to effectively deliver projects. The specialists within HR can sometimes fail to realise that effective project execution as an important competence, so if numbers of staff are being pared back, then the benefits of retaining project management skills can go unnoticed.

Such turnovers in staff can also have an unintended side-effect. People are brought into an organisation to give a fresh perspective and to offer new expertise. However, new arrivals in a role quite often go through a lifecycle of being critical of what went before. A syndrome of 'not done where I used to work, and where I used to work, we did this better' can arise. This means that knowledge may be dismissed and overlooked, so that corporate learnings need to be relearnt and mistakes sometimes run the risk of being repeated.

One of the key ways to minimise this effect is to make sure that where structured rulebooks for project management are developed, everyone is made aware of them and trained in them to the level that makes sense for them. This will vary depending upon the extent of their involvement in project management. The aim, though, should be that this awareness becomes both widespread and deep-seated. As a result, it will become the 'way we do things around here' and this will mean that the organisation's expertise in project management will be resilient to most types of organisational change.

A possible way to introduce project thinking into the business would be to arrange for certain regular business activities to be undertaken using a project paradigm. A good candidate for such an exercise would be the preparation of the annual budget. The person from the business would then learn about project concepts in the context of a business activity with which they were already familiar. At a later date, if they were involved with a project, some of the project concepts would be familiar, which would help the business and project to speak the same language.

The final human aspect that needs to be considered is stress. It is very rare to find a stress-free project. A whole range of reasons, many already discussed in this book, can lead to problems which will result in stress for the project team. This often leads to working extended days (and nights). This can be a double-edged sword, as long hours can impair people's judgement, leading to over-reactions to the wrong things and the wrong choices being made in decisions.

In addition, problems and stress can also lead to overworked and stretched project teams. These often do not have the correctly skilled resources and may have to assign the person most closely skilled to a task. This may in theory give the best chance of trying to stick to the schedule, but may also result in slower or poorer-quality output. However, there is no easy answer, since waiting to get the right resource might delay the project too much.

Key Points

- The organisational structure for 'business as usual' functions tends to have a different flavour from that of a project.

- The business organisation chart is often fixed and stable for a business cycle (quite often a financial year).

- Restructures might be regular, but will also be predictable.

- The HR function will take a people-centric view of the organisation rather than a view influenced by process, finance or technology.

- The HR function will have a role to play in a project both in terms of staffing-up an in-house project team and also in relation to helping to make any organisational changes that a project might deliver happen.

- People from the business can be dropped into the deep end of a project without enough background briefing.

- They may retain 'business as usual' responsibilities which may not fit well with project demands, leading to significant stress.

- The key feature of a project is that it is forever fluid, evolving and never the same in terms of structure and post-holders for more than a couple of weeks.

- People who work in the project world have a different style of career path from 'business as usual' staff.

- The timeline for recruitment of project staff is shorter than for 'business as usual' staff.

- Project people often aim for a bigger assignment and more responsibility on each successive project.

- Project people often consider that they are going to be judged on getting the project done, maybe at the expense of relationships and stepping on a few toes.

- Being in a project team can be quite painful if the individual is forever going from one stressful late-running project to another.

- To bridge the divide, both parties need to understand the points made above and consider the following:

  - co-locate business and project staff and, where possible, create mixed teams so that barriers do not necessarily evolve in the first place;
  - if the schedules will permit it, it can be useful for members of the business to spend a few days shadowing someone in the project and then vice versa;

- where a project and a business have induction programmes for their respective staff, send business people on the project induction course and vice versa;
- generate awareness in each party of the other's viewpoints and the over-riding need to act as a single unified team;
- consider training wherever possible;
- even if it is not possible to co-locate all of the team, it is still well worth trying to minimise geographical separation;
- take a step back and design a coherent and cohesive set of norms, and reward structures, that cover both the business and the project;
- arrange opportunities for socialising together;
- be aware of the complexities and subtleties of the internal structures for both the business and the project teams;
- attempt to minimise the isolation caused by a silo mentality;
- take action to guard against knowledge loss due to staff turnover;
- be sensitive to stress levels and that different people will react to the same level of challenge in radically different ways.

Having explored the 'softer' side of the business, now let us next turn to the most quantitative – finance.

Chapter 14

Finance

The distinction in viewpoint between the business community and the project community is at its most pronounced when finance is considered.

The Business Perspective

For the business, a certain number of classic features are central to the way in which finance works and is thought about. The most significant aspect is the nature of patterns, cycles and repeatability.

All businesses run against an annual cycle of financial events. Each year a budget will be set, performance tracked and reported against the budget, and then this outcome will be used to inform how the budget will be set for the following year. The result of the annual cycle is that there are predictable periods when particular activities will occur: budget setting, budget approvals, tracking of performance on a monthly, quarterly, half-yearly and annual basis. All organisations have a requirement to report their finances on an annual basis, while many public quoted companies will also have to give half-yearly reports, and for larger ones potentially also quarterly reports.

A number of these activities will run in parallel, particularly in the lead-up to and the immediate aftermath of a year-end.

This pattern of work will be deeply ingrained within the business overall, and be woven so fundamentally into the mindset of the finance function that they would be surprised to discover that anyone was not aware of it. The impact of this is that, on a monthly basis, days, maybe a week or two, are given over to the activities of tracking and reporting the finances for the business. This makes the finance team less available and potentially only able to contribute to project activities during the other two to three weeks of the month. When the month-end falls at a quarter, half or full year boundary, the duration of this

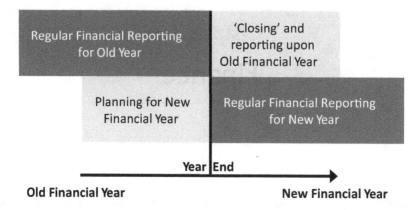

Figure 14.1   Financial activities around year-end

unavailability may start sooner and will certainly last longer. To the business, the fact that the members of the finance team, and to some extent the senior management who need to review their output and make decisions based upon it, can only contribute during their available periods is self-evident. They would assume that all project team members would automatically know this and factor it into their plans.

This periodicity also has another side-effect. It both drives and constrains project deadlines. The business may require the project to put its solution into operation in line with a significant financial boundary – a half-year or full-year-end. At the same time, in other circumstances, the available time-slots for when a solution can go live are often restricted, with the half-year and year-end time periods leading to closed seasons when the financial processes are so critical that the business cannot risk the potential disruption of the change that the project is planning to deliver. Potentially it could not survive the impact of the change going wrong or failing, and the project not being able to reinstate the previous arrangements quickly and smoothly.

The financial mindset will also affect the lens through which members of the finance community think about the project. An affinity and comfort with a very quantitative way of viewing the world, particularly converting everything into a financial value, means that this part of the business will take what may feel like a very narrow view of the project.

The finance function will play a key part in the business case for getting the project up and running. Their expertise may be needed to create the business case in the first place. They may well set the rules about the amount of payback the project should achieve and how long it has to achieve it. They can determine how the benefits that the project is planning to deliver will be valued financially, and as a result whether it will meet the relevant benchmarks for getting funding. They may be essential players in the management forums that release the money needed by the project. They might be involved in comparing a number of projects that are all competing for the same allocation of finance. Sometimes they can come across as particularly detached and overly analytical, which can clash with the passion and enthusiasm of the team involved in getting the project up and running. In general, they may take a less 'touchy feely' approach to business change and obtaining buy-in. In particular, if a project needs to restructure a business and as a result some people lose their jobs, the finance team may appear cold and hard-hearted, particularly if they characterise staff as costs and give the impression that they do not see the employees as real people.

It is worth considering that although superficially some aspects of the 'finance culture' may feel similar to the project culture, there are other dimensions that can be quite different. One aspect of this is the use of time recording, often via timesheets. Almost all projects do this as a matter of course so as to be able to track their expenditure of effort for each area of activity. The finance function will be very familiar with such practices, but in some cases may not work in the same way. It is less common to find an in-house finance function that uses timesheets, and so if they are included into a project team whose members are required to record their time, they may not be particularly comfortable with this practice.

One other area of surprise can relate to the use of technology. Finance functions were one of the first parts of the business world to adopt technology (with data processing as it then was), being extensive users of computers decades before other parts of a business. However, this familiarity and reliance on technology does not necessarily translate into a detailed appreciation of the steps involved in a project to create or upgrade this technology. Each specialism tends to have its own ways of working, which other disciplines sometimes regard as bureaucratic or excessively pedantic. In the same way as many people outside finance find it fairly impenetrable and jargon-ridden, so the finance community, unless time is taken to explain the project process, can be equally impatient about the steps that a project team needs to follow to achieve a successful delivery. In effect, the project can see the finance department as only worrying about the numbers and not being sympathetic to the technical challenges faced by the project, which might change, delay or derail it.

But on the other side of the fence, finance functions can also feel unloved. This perception can stem from a variety of causes, including that they are simply the part of the business that 'keeps the score' rather than the part that 'plays the game and wins the points'. Other viewpoints can include that they hold the purse strings to change and unless a positive financial case can be proven, they can stand in the way of making a change that others view as beneficial. These presumptions can affect the way in which members of the project team view the finance function and can lead to misunderstandings that reduce the effectiveness of the joint working relationship.

The Project Perspective

The project approach to financial matters can be quite different. The first scenario arises when finances are not even considered. Innovative projects that do not need too much effort in terms of time and people, at least in their early days, sometimes get started without any allocated budget. They borrow resources from other activities, which may suffer as a result, or occasionally get team members to work in their 'free time' – lunchtimes, evenings and weekends – if they are passionate enough about the endeavour. These various arrangements are often termed 'skunkworks', where pre-existing resources get borrowed, sometime visibly and sometimes with a degree of subterfuge. There can be legitimate reasons to do this: sometimes it is just not possible to prove a business case to get a project approved and funded, while sometimes even if the money is there, the right resources may not be available. In order to overcome this barrier, an approach of 'let's get started and build something anyway' prevails, with the intention of creating a demonstrable early version of the eventual solution. This is done with the belief that once the business and the potential backers of the project can actually see the capability and benefits that the solution can provide, they will swing in behind the project, provide some funding and enable it to ramp-up to a much larger project that will then create the full solution. At this point, the project stops side-stepping finance and almost does an 'about-turn' so that it is in a position whereby it needs to follow the formal paths to obtain the full allocation of money that it needs so that it can set itself up properly as a formal project.

At times, even when a project is properly funded, the financial disciplines can get overlooked in the early days. This classic scenario is similar to a university student getting their student loan (or for older UK readers their Grant Cheque) at the start of term and then trying to budget for 10 weeks and not burn through all the money in the first fortnight. At the start of a project, the budget allocated can sometimes seem large enough that it would be hard to imagine spending it all, and the concept of a run-rate of weekly spending may feel too boring and constraining. As a result, project expenditure can rapidly escalate without enough control and before the project knows it, it is 20 per cent of its way through its schedule and creation of deliverables, but it has unintentionally already used 40 per cent of its budget.

This is why some more experienced project managers can be particularly tight with the project finances, to the surprise of the rest of their project team and sometimes also the business. The most effective technique is one of regularly re-estimating the cost to complete. Done most thoroughly, this involves looking at every task that remains to be done in the project, how much effort is going to be expended upon it, how much each resource working on that task costs and then for all other expenditure on materials, services and expenses, how much of that is also required to undertake all of the remaining tasks. An insightful project manager will not assume that the set of remaining tasks simply equals those in the original plan minus those already finished. They will precede the estimate with an analysis of how the project is going, making sure that the plan to complete includes any new tasks that have arisen since the original plan was put together. These may be needed as a result of scope changes, because the timeline slipped and extra activities are needed to bring it back on schedule, or because some tasks were overlooked in the original planning, or because of problems arising with the project they are now required. These all need to be factored into the mix to get the cost to complete. This can be further complicated if the schedule has slipped markedly and, as a result, the cost of resources has gone up. The same amount of effort by the same resource to undertake a task might now cost the project more than was predicted in the original plan. All of this is used to gain a true picture of how much it is really likely to cost to finish the project. This activity concentrates the mind wonderfully and is likely to result in a focused and motivated project manager who will be keen to drive the project team to a timely completion of their work. If this is repeated regularly, at least monthly, then the chances of the project experiencing a nasty surprise or veering expensively off-course are significantly reduced.

Bridging the Divide

The intersection between project finance and business finance processes can overlay, distort and disrupt regular 'business as usual' finance activities. It can also make project financial processes more confusing and less agile than sometimes they need to be. For instance, the finance function will usually have an interface with the project in terms of the cost-tracking environment, but can often be rather adrift or unaligned to the project's financial tracking approach. To overcome this, the two teams need to come together near the start of the project and first identify and explain to each other what their regular processes are. This should then be followed by analysis that highlights where the processes interact, both in a positive way and also how they might hinder each other, for instance, slow turnaround on purchase approvals or inability to obtain real-time access to time and effort data. This can sometimes be exacerbated if parallel accounting worlds develop, with project costs being held and tracked in a project financial spreadsheet that needs regular reconciliation with the main corporate accounting systems.

Handling change effectively can help bridge the divide. Once a project is off and running, it almost always encounters change of some sort. This usually results in a series of change requests. Unless a very clear approach is kept to requirements and scope management by the business, and to cost allocation against work items by the project, there are real risks here. Such change requests can quickly give rise to confusion in terms of budget status and progress against budget. One area that is quite common relates to delays in getting approvals which can lead to the project 'working at risk', i.e. getting started on a task before the business has agreed whether it will fund the task. This is done on the expectation that the funding will be agreed pretty quickly and that, given the pressures required for the work, the project would be delayed and disrupted too much if the start of the work had to wait until all of the change control process was followed and completed. This can lead to mix-ups when it becomes hard to reconcile work against approved and unapproved spend. Was the extra money available or not? In this situation, developing a slick set of working processes that enable changes to be rapidly assessed and either quickly approved or declined can help minimise this risk of funding confusion.

Closely related to this challenge is one whereby a series, even a backlog, of change requests starts to arise. It is not uncommon for funding to undertake early stages of change requests to not be available. This means that project effort and budget is used to review and size-up a Change Request, and, in particular, if the change request then does not go ahead, this funding is no longer available for the original work which still needs doing. If the change requests are only a small fraction of the project, this may be tolerable; however, if a large number of change requests arise and a substantial proportion of them are not taken forwards, then the project could find its funding position materially damaged.

Another area that can undermine a project can come from an unexpected angle. Although the finances of a project are generally assured once it is off and running, provided that it sticks to its agreed budget, it is likely to be reliant on support services from a range of business functions. If financial pressures in the main business lead to restructurings, these support services may get reconfigured, or may even disappear at comparatively short notice. It is important that the project makes clear to the business that although it sometimes behaves as an island, in practice it actually relies upon a number of key 'business as usual' services – including HR, purchasing, finance, general IT and similar activities. A sudden curtailment of these will cost the project money whilst it finds alternative ways to meet its needs, which themselves may cost more, so that the savings the business thinks it may be achieving by restructuring could be reduced as a result of such unintended consequences.

The last point meriting consideration is that of multiple funding sources. Sometimes a project will be financed from a range of sources either across the business or from more than one business. This can have the result of making it need to report to more than one master, potentially with conflicting requirements and priorities. This can inhibit the start-up of the work, which may need to wait for all funders to be in place. It can also destabilise the smooth progress of the project, as the continual need to reconcile and integrate the competing and contrasting views of the disparate funders will take time and energy, and may lead to a loss of clarity and focus in the deliverables. It can also lead to the rug being pulled out from under the project's feet quite suddenly if one or more of the key funders either wishes to or has to withdraw from supporting the project.

In summary, although both finance functions and projects teams tend to have a structured mindset, they do not necessarily think the same way. So the key technique remains communication between the project and the finance community. This may not always be easy, but time and effort invested in it will reap dividends.

Key Points

- Businesses run against an annual cycle of financial events.

- This pattern of work will be deeply ingrained within the business overall and will be woven so fundamentally into the mindset of the finance function that they would be surprised to discover that anyone was not aware of it.

- This periodicity both drives and constrains project deadlines.

- The finance part of the business will take what may feel like a very narrow view of the project.

- These people will also play a key part in the business case for the project.

- The finance function's familiarity and reliance on technology does not necessarily translate into a detailed appreciation of the steps involved in a project to create or upgrade this technology.

- The project can see the finance department as only worrying about the numbers and not being sympathetic to the technical challenges faced by the project.

- For some early-stage innovative projects, finances may not even be considered.

- Within a project, financial disciplines can get overlooked in the early days.

- The most effective technique is one of regularly re-estimating the cost to complete the project.

- To bridge the divide, both parties need to understand the points made above and consider the following:

  - the two teams need to come together near the start of the project and first identify and explain to each other what their regular processes are;
  - develop a slick set of working processes that enable changes to be rapidly assessed and either quickly approved or declined can help minimise risk;
  - the project needs to makes clear to the business that although it sometimes behaves as an island, in practice it relies upon a number of 'business as usual' services – including HR, purchasing, finance, general IT and similar activities;

- achieve a joint appreciation that being financed from a range of sources either across the business or from more than one business can give the project more than one master, potentially with conflicting requirements and priorities;
- realise and acknowledge that although both finance functions and projects teams tend to have a structured mindset, they do not necessarily think the same way.

Chapter 15

Reporting

The essence of reporting is to provide the information necessary in order to monitor performance and, where necessary, take action as a result. The project and the business approaches to this can differ quite significantly.

The Business Perspective

Business reporting tends to follow one of two patterns. The first pattern relates to the nature of the core operational processes that the business follows. If they are quick and high volume, then the reporting activity may in effect be real-time and continual. If the business is has a longer 'cycle time', maybe producing a new product once a week, then reporting will reflect that. Once a business process is well established, it will in general perform satisfactorily, and so the reporting about it will probably be tracking minor variations in its effectiveness. It will be related to managing success, how close the output is to the expected target and whether the business has beaten its quota for this month.

The second pattern will be anchored in the financial cycles of the business; as discussed in earlier chapters, reports will reflect the annual, half-yearly and other financial periods that the business uses to plan and manage its performance. Again, there will be an expectation that the business will operate reasonably closely to its budget. A variation of plus or minus 20 per cent would feel significant. Unless the market moves suddenly and unexpectedly against the business, it would normally not expect to diverge wildly and at short notice from its predicted financial performance.

In contrast, project reporting may feel alien to the business. It is different from day-to-day 'business as usual' reporting, which is continually tracking performance month-in, month-out against a set of well-defined performance targets. The project is not a continuous process that is being reported upon, but a one-off activity with a set of lifecycle stages. Progress through this lifecycle is rarely smooth and so progress reporting much more often talks about problems. This can feel odd, negative and counter-cultural when compared to classic business reports.

The way in which project reporting is provided to the business will make a difference. Within the business there are multiple audiences comprising individuals, committees and possibly boards. All of these will want some level of reporting. Some of them meet infrequently, taking a strategic viewpoint. They tend to have long lead-times for the provision of information into them. This may not suit a project as it is often fast moving and the status from two or three weeks ago is no longer relevant to the project as circumstances may already have moved on. These different audiences will want varying levels of detail and will have different start points; as a result, a report developed for one audience will not meet the needs of a different audience. This means that the project may need to come up with multiple reports, in theory all talking about the same time period, but in practice discussing it at different levels. This can be quite demanding upon the project, both in terms of the level of effort needed to produce all these reports and also in terms of making sure that they are all consistent and that they do not diverge over time.

From the viewpoint of the business, project reporting can appear excessive, bureaucratic and confusing. If the business is not familiar with projects, then the style of reporting may not be as accessible and comprehensible as it needs to be. This can lead to the business gaining a poor impression of the project. Sometimes it is not obvious what progress has been made. In other situations, if there is a lot of bad news, the reporting process can feel like a litany of excuses.

The business can be faced with an additional challenge. Where there are projects running in organisations without a project support culture, they will have to develop their reporting styles and formats from scratch. If there are a number of projects from different teams and suppliers running at the same time, this can lead to multiple inconsistent reporting approaches, using variable terminology, making it harder for the business to understand, gain a strategic overview and assess comparative performance.

All of this may feel unfair to the project. There is, however, one scenario where the business needs to take particular care. If there is a particularly toxic project, which has run into deep trouble, members of the project team can end up focusing a lot of effort on dodging blame rather than explaining facts. If people in the business have been on the receiving end of one or more of these types of project, their general perception of project reporting may be heavily skewed against giving the next project they encounter the benefit of the doubt.

The Project Perspective

In the project world, however, reporting is the key to controlling a project effectively. It serves two purposes: first, making sure that project management knows what is happening so that it can direct activity and take remedial action where needed; and, second, providing a structured conversation with the sponsors, clients and recipients of the project's work.

For a project, the ability to report effectively depends upon whether a good set of tools and a support environment is in place. This comprises the ability to easily gain a comprehensive picture of the time and effort being expended by the project team, as well as tracking what needs to be purchased and what individual expenses are being incurred.

For larger projects, with many teams, workstreams and possibly different geographies, the assembly and validation of data can introduce delays into the reporting process, meaning that a weekly report, by the time it is ready to be published, is already a week out of date.

Bringing all of this information together quickly and efficiently so that a real-time picture can be established at the end of each week is the secret to the project being able to know where it is, how it has got to this place and where it will be heading. This then allows it to ask questions along the lines of whether it is still within the agreed boundaries of time, cost and scope or quality. Building upon this, it then needs to consider whether its direction of travel will get it to its intended destination or whether adjustments to the route, team, funding or methods are needed to bring it back on course.

Time and cost are easier to track and quantify, so they tend to be the default forms of reporting. The challenge that projects face is how to measure, analyse and convey this information in a way that is meaningful and enables real insight to be made quickly and easily. Complications can ensue when there are varying baselines for comparison. The project then needs to be clear what it is that the report is measuring progress against.

One complication regarding financial reporting can be that the financial systems used by the business to run its day-to-day operations may not be suitable for project reporting. In particular, the coding scheme may not be designed to capture important categories of project expenditure. In addition, the system might not be able to capture and report upon expenditure spread across a number of financial years. If this arises, then the project team may develop its own set of financial tracking mechanisms, usually a set of complex spreadsheets. In these circumstances two parallel accounting worlds can develop: the project finance world and the business finance world. Extra effort is then needed to keep these reconciled and aligned. If this is not done, the true cost of the project starts to become uncertain.

Progress in the creation of deliverables, and in the level of quality, is sometimes harder to quantify. A pressurised project may find that focus can fall disproportionately on time and cost, with not enough attention being paid to quality.

Bridging the Divide

There are a number of useful techniques to bring the parties together. As with other areas, communication is central.

Effective meetings will help. A 'one team culture' rather than a 'them and us' approach, where the client and the project are at loggerheads, can only be beneficial. This will be aided by having a good agenda and working practices. These can be supported by a proper structure for governance meetings, with clarity on who attends, their levels in the organisations, the frequency of the meetings and the balancing of the agendas. Being clear about roles and authority limits (sometimes set by the wider organisation) in terms of who can do what without having to refer upwards will enable meetings to make decisions where they can, and will not waste time when they cannot. In particular, it is worth trying to keep progress, problems, fault diagnosis, remedial action and blame separate so that arguments are avoided.

This situation works best where all the facts are available in a timely manner and they can be understood by all the parties. There are techniques that can be very valuable in communicating complex information relating to progress in a way that is quick and easily comprehensible. For instance, diagrammatic dependency chain charts which can be colour-coded to show progress are a good way of demonstrating how everything is fitting together and progressing.

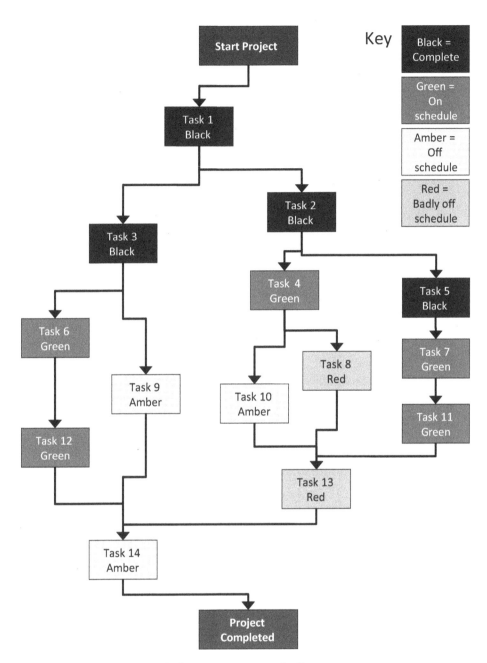

Figure 15.1   Colour-coded progress network diagram

Milestone trend analysis charts, which can give a realistic indication of likely future outcomes, are also very useful. An Internet search will yield a number of vendors of tools that can draw these charts.

Both of these techniques are better than Gantt charts. The nature and history of Gantt charts is explained by Wilson (2003). However, although valuable for planning, Gantt charts tend to be confusing for reporting and can make it hard to discern the big picture and overall trends.

One other aspect to consider is how the range of problems that can beset a project will manifest themselves via the reporting process:

- Time zones – both the project and the business need to beware of delays if multi-time zone work gets out of sync and delays, sized in days per week, start to stack up.

- Excess auditing – even if it is on an even keel, a project can quite often be subject to a range of audit activities. Flavours of auditor can include financial, computer security, quality, health and safety, risk – the list can go on. All will have different perspectives and agendas; each on their own would not cause too much trouble, but together they can overload a successful project. It should be part of the activities of the senior team monitoring the project's progress reports to make sure that it is not being overly distracted by audits. If the project runs into trouble, the volume of reviews and audits can ramp-up in an attempt to understand what has gone wrong and propose solutions. Again, a balance needs to be struck so that the judicious use of reviews will be key to recovering the project rather than further swamping it.

- Projects that are in trouble sometimes de-prioritise client communication so as not to share bad news and to focus on trying to recover from the problem situation: 'Don't talk about the problems, we can fix them, then we'll update the client'. In fact, increasing communication is more likely to maintain client confidence, treating them as adults, having to 'take the flak', whereas radio silence can increase levels of client worry and provoke a reduction in trust.

- A sign of ineffective reporting, which may involve closing the stable door after the horse has bolted, is when a drip-drip-drip of a problem finally leads to the dam bursting and a major problem arising. It can take a crisis before a problem in a project is fully recognized. Conversely, sometimes these are easier to recover from as there is more impetus to take the necessary corrective action.

- Fixing problems can involve a wide variety of steps and challenges. When a project is facing problems, fixing a few things quickly and visibly, and embedding the fix so that it endures for more than just a few weeks, will be more effective than a long laundry list of slowly implemented remedial actions.

If the worst comes to the worst, sometimes the relationship between the business and the project can become so toxic that the best route is to abandon the project, attempt to learn the lessons, have a pause, get a new team, start again or even see if changes in the landscape during the intervening period have negated the need for the project completely. This is not ideal, but on rare occasions it may be necessary to take such action as the project otherwise will just spiral down and throw good money after bad. However, if the approaches considered in this book are adopted, the chances of reaching this state will be greatly reduced.

Key Points

- 'Business as usual' reporting tends to be related to production or service processes and managing their success, how close the output is to the expected target and whether the business has beaten its quota for this month.

- There is also a second pattern of business reporting that will be anchored in the financial cycles of the business.

- From the viewpoint of the business, project reporting can appear excessive, bureaucratic and confusing.

- Project progress through its lifecycle is rarely smooth, and so project progress reporting much more often talks about problems. This can feel odd, negative and counter-cultural when compared to classic business reports.

- If there are a number of projects from different teams and suppliers running at the same time, this can lead to multiple inconsistent reporting approaches, using variable terminology.

- A project is often fast moving and the status from two or three weeks ago is usually no longer relevant to the project as circumstances may already have moved on.

- In the project world, however, reporting is the key to controlling a project effectively.

- For larger projects, the assembly and validation of data can introduce delays into the reporting process.

- Time and cost are easier to track and quantify, so they tend to be the default forms of reporting.

- Progress in the creation of deliverables, and in the level of quality, is sometimes harder to quantify.

- To bridge the divide, both parties need to understand the points made above and consider the following:

  - a 'one team culture' rather than a 'them and us' approach where the client and project are at loggerheads, can only be beneficial;
  - agree preferred understandable reporting formats (potentially diagrammatic) and use them consistently;
  - beware of projects with problems in relation to multiple time-zone working, excessive audit burdens, reductions in client communications, and reporting that seeks to minimise significant challenges and risks.

Chapter 16
Benefits

This book could legitimately have started with a discussion on benefits. They are the raison d'etre of a project, but, interestingly, business and project viewpoints and approaches to this aspect of projects can vary.

The Business Perspective

From the business' viewpoint, achieving benefits are why the business did the project. The central question that the business tends to focus on is: 'Will it achieve the intended benefits?' This is not always as obvious to determine as it might seem. For one thing, the business, as has been highlighted already, is in reality composed of a number of different functions. The operations, HR and finance teams will all view this differently. Operations may be happy that the project has achieved its objective, provided that it delivers the required solution, while for HR, the human change dimension – achieving successful buy-in and new ways of working – will be most important; however, for finance, a clear payback with an acceptable return on investment will be the only benchmark that truly enables a project to demonstrate that it has provided benefits.

The business can have a central role to play in putting the deliverables the project provides into action and realising a working solution. For this to happen, the project will sometimes drive the business to take structured action to change the way it works. This will tend to involve a need to identify timelines for actions, key responsibilities, changes to processes and changes to the structure of the organisation. This may or may not fit with what the business was expecting and its ability to make this change happen. It will need to address considerations, including new work tasks, different ways to undertake existing tasks or stopping certain work activities. The business will be at the heart of determining how these changes will combine and when they will take effect. The business will also need to be clear on who makes the changes and who tracks that the changes have happened.

Once the changes have happened, measurement will be needed to assess whether they have had the desired effect. There are many different business-related finance figures to be brought together, new systems, potential redundancy costs and varying accounting conventions, all of which need to be factored into the benefit calculations.

One other point that may need to be taken into consideration relates to a scenario where there is an 'internal market' in benefits, with many projects all trying to lay claim to the same savings, in which case a central arbitration function may be required to adjudicate between competing projects and determine which ones have actually made a difference.

As this book has noted on a number of occasions, projects themselves almost always experience considerable change. This will also need to be taken into consideration. Under such circumstances, the business will also need to ask how this compares to the original plan and what else has changed during the life of the project. Only by having a clear grasp of these features of the landscape will a true benefits assessment be possible.

The Project Perspective

The project perspective on benefits may be quite at odds with the business. In its shortest form, it may consist of: 'Go live, get it working, close down the snagging list'.

In practice, the attitude of the project towards benefits will very much depend upon whether the project or the business has responsibility for benefits realisation. If the project simply provides some technology and it has been agreed upfront that the business will be responsible for making sure that the technology is put into use, then the project is likely to be very 'hands-off' in relation to benefits. If, however, the project can only declare itself complete and maybe only then can receive its final payments, after the benefits are demonstrated to have been achieved, then the project will not only stay involved but it is also likely to be very proactive about making sure that the benefits are realised. In some cases this may be more difficult, depending upon how quickly the benefits will arrive after the go-live event(s). If there is a gap of a number of months or even years, then the project will probably morph into a different shape, with the technology delivery strand falling away, but with a business change team still present and very much becoming the centre of its focus.

Bridging the Divide

So how can these two perspectives be brought together? Considering the practical process of identifying, measuring and making changes to realise the planned benefits will provide the best way to unite the viewpoints. It is necessary for clarity to be established first as to who has responsibility and accountability for benefits. Then a range of factors needs to be examined.

Timelines and quantification come first. This involves making sure that a clear quantified picture is established of the 'before world'. Negotiations may well be needed to agree what should be measured, and care will be needed not to distort the areas under scrutiny simply as a result of measuring them. Where possible, the data to be used should be collected as a byproduct of a pre-existing process, as this will reduce the chances that it is concocted simply to make the starting point look bad. The timeline element is also significant in that if data is not collected in 'real time' before the project gets started, there may be a paucity of information once the change has got underway. If the need to undertake such measurement only hits the collective consciousness of the project team a while after the project has got underway, the benefits work may be forced to rely on 'archaeology' and sift through data about the old way of working that may be incomplete and not directly relevant. Having to use this data to reconstruct a quantified picture of the start point is not good, but if that is all that is available, then it should still be done, as a comparison must have two sets of data to be meaningful.

This book has mentioned many times that projects are often instigated as a result of changes and are also constructed themselves to result in change. One inevitable consequence of this situation is that any given project of any appreciable length will not be the only change agent within an environment in a particular period of time. Whilst the project is underway, the landscape around and underneath it may also be changing for a range of possible reasons and causes. These reasons are not so important here, but what does matter is that it then makes it harder to ascribe a beneficial outcome to the project if a number of other accidental upheavals and deliberate change initiatives are also happening in parallel. In such circumstances, great care will need to be taken to demonstrate that the changes that are manifest at the end of the project can legitimately be attributed to the project, and not to one of the other sources of change.

If the project team is not directly responsible for the benefits element, then the business will need to take deliberate steps to make sure that certain roles, and probably identifiable individual post-holders, can be assigned the task of making sure that the ongoing tracking of benefit data continues for the desired time period to enable a complete enough data-set to be gathered, so that the realisation or otherwise of the benefits can be assessed.

Throughout all of this, particular care and caution needs to be applied. There are a number of pitfalls that can trip up the unwary:

- Certain individuals may be incentivised to 'game' the benefits measurement process and focus on the changes that are needed to meet agreed target values, which may be achievable without actually making the intended underlying real changes.

- If a number of projects end up needing to be compared to get a combined view of their collective benefit, then this will add an additional complication since statistics to assess the success of different projects are often collected in different ways so that it can be really quite difficult to 'compare apples with apples'.

- Sometimes, although there are no other major changes happening at the same time as a project, the data being measured can be subject to background variations, e.g. due to economic activity or the weather. It will be necessary to strip out such background variation across time so as to establish a consistent and solid reference point from which to measure the impact of the change.

- Although a project can easily think that it is in a world of its own, more often than not, there are other parallel projects also making changes. In some cases these projects in effect compete to improve the same area or set of processes. As a result, benefits can be sometimes claimed by multiple projects across a single organisation. To counter this, first the situation needs to be spotted and then a central clearing house and arbitration mechanism is needed to combine the claimed benefits, remove double counting and allocate them fairly to the project or projects that have had the greatest impact.

- Finally, it is quite common for business users to change over the lifetime of a project. As new post-holders take up their roles, the project team can be knocked off-course. What they thought of as 'agreed benefits' can become 'un-agreed' when new business users take over and are not aware of or choose not to recognise or ratify the previously agreed benefits.

Key Points

* From the business' viewpoint, achieving benefits are why the business did the project.

* The business can have a central role to play in putting the deliverables the project provides into action and realising a working solution.

* Once the changes have happened, measurement will be needed to assess whether they have had the desired effect.

* In its shortest form, the project view may consist of: 'Go live, get it working, close down the snagging list'.

* The project's view of benefits will very much depend upon whether the project or the business has responsibility for benefits realisation. It is possible that each party will think it is the other one's responsibility.

* To bridge the divide, both parties need to understand the points made above and consider the following:

  – making sure that a clear quantified picture is established of the 'before world';
  – taking care to demonstrate that the changes that are manifest at the end of the project can legitimately be attributed to the project and not to another source of change;
  – agreeing how these activities will be done before effort is expended upon them.

Further Reading

This chapter has deliberately only skimmed the surface of the topic of benefits. There is a new 'classic' book (Jenner 2012) that has recently been published about this theme. For readers wanting a deeper treatment of this area, it provides a comprehensive discussion of the subject.

Chapter 17
Conclusions

So how do we bring this all together? What conclusions can be drawn from the discussions relating to the gap between business and projects?

The gap may be a gap of culture, of understanding or of attitude and habit. The awareness of the differences in terms of culture and the understanding of work processes and approach have hopefully been reduced as a result of reading this book. The dimensions of attitude and habit are slightly different.

It is worth reflecting that, in general, across the business and project communities, good practice on how to run effective projects is well known. So why is it not followed? The reasons span a range of factors, which will combine to different degrees in each situation:

- Fear – often stemming from competition whether explicit or implicit. A culture whereby the project team members feel that they are at risk in some way if the project does not deliver can be stimulating if carefully constructed and well bounded. An environment that is more hostile, where competition and serious consequences have arisen almost by accident, can push both parties into ways of working that do not support a constructive approach to each other. Effort becomes invested in protecting one's back, potentially at the expense of the other party, and, as a result, any hopes of partnership degenerate into a corrosive conflict between the two camps that diverts creativity and energy away from working together and saps morale and optimism, leaving a set of cynical and uninspired participants.

- Lack of interest – this may seem almost trivial, but it can have significant consequences. One person's attention to detail is another's pointless bureaucracy. A mismatch between styles of thinking and working, particularly if one party has a collective tendency to be more cavalier whilst the other is more risk averse, can result in a failure to achieve a meeting of minds, which again dooms the project to repeated frustration and misunderstandings.

- Over-optimism – surely optimism is a good thing to have in a project? Without it, the project is on a route to despondency and pessimism. Although true, the key word here is 'over'. Being too positive can lead to arrogance and hubris. This can manifest itself as a blind faith that the project will succeed, without the realism and humility to appreciate that a successful outcome can rarely be taken for granted.

- Personal biases – no one is unbiased, but appreciating one's own viewpoint can be quite difficult. If one is unaware of one's own biases, one will not notice the consequences. People instinctively focus on what they are interested in. They will do a good job on the tasks that relate to what they value and enjoy. They will inadvertently skimp and give less attention to the work that does not attract them. Most people tend not to be particularly aware of their own blindspots, so they may not realise they are even doing this. If the collective culture of either party is too strong and consistent, then the same blindspots may be shared by many in the team, and either party in the project may find that it is consistently valuing and focusing on some aspects and neglecting other elements of the project.

- Incentives – these can drive the behaviours that will make the key difference. Some incentives will have been carefully designed, while others may have arisen simply by accident. Irrespective of their start point, the impact will be the same. Incentives aligned to achieving a shared approach, a common vision and a constructive partnering attitude will help to foster a success project. Incentives that skew behaviour in the direct of particular types of activity, neglecting other areas of work, and that prioritise selfishness and a me-first instinct within either party are likely to increase rather than reduce levels of misunderstanding and conflict.

To address these challenges, both the business and the project need to be actively aware of the risks of fear, lack of interest, over-optimism, personal biases and poor incentives. By taking time to consider these dimensions and their interplay with the lifecycle stages and through-project strands that this book has discussed, a self-aware and informed approach can be taken to establishing and maintaining a culture that will bridge the business and project divide.

In reality, the bridge does not need to be built – it is actually already there. To close the gap, both parties simply need to make a deliberate effort to walk across it as often as they can, to stand on the other side of the divide and look at the situation from the other party's point of view.

Bibliography

Some of the references below are mentioned in the text of the book; others are listed here as they are valuable sources of additional insights into the worlds of project management and business as usual, which have informed my thinking on the interplay between the two perspectives.

APM Body of Knowledge, 6th edn. Princes Risborough: Association for Project Management, 2013.

Beck, K. et al. 'Manifesto for Agile Software Development', 2001. Available at: http://agilemanifesto.org.

Bignell, V. and Fortune, J. *Understanding Systems Failures*. Manchester: Manchester University Press, 1984.

Carnall, C. *Managing Change in Organizations*. Hemel Hempstead: Prentice Hall Europe, 1995.

Carter, R., Martin, J., Mayblin, B. and Munday, M. *Systems, Management and Change*. London: Harper & Row, 1985.

Chambers, A.D., Selim, G.M. and Vinten, G. *Internal Auditing*. London: Pitman Publishing, 1987.

Driver, P.M. *Validating Strategies*. Farnham: Gower, 2014.

DSDM Atern v2, The Handbook. Ashford: DSDM Consortium, 2008.

Fowler, A. and Lock, D. *Accelerating Business and IT Change: Transforming Project Delivery*. Farnham: Gower, 2006.

Graves, T. *Enterprise Architecture*. Ely: IT Governance Publishing, 2009.

A Guide to the Project Management Body of Knowledge (PMBOK® Guide) – Fifth Edition. Newtown Square, PA: Project Management Institute, 2013.

Hamer, M. and Champy, J. *Reengineering the Corporation*. London: Nicholas Brealey Publishing, 1997.

Handy, C.B. *Understanding Organisations*. Harmondsworth: Penguin, 1985.

Handy, C.B. *The Age of Unreason*. London: Business Books, 1989.

Jenner, S. *Managing Benefits*. Norwich: TSO (The Stationery Office) for the APM Group Limited, 2012.

Jones, C. *Patterns of Software Systems Failure and Success*. Boston, MA: International Thomson Computer Press, 1996.

Managing Successful Programmes 2011 Edition. Norwich: TSO (The Stationery Office) for AXELOS Ltd, 2011.

Managing Successful Projects with PRINCE2™ 2009 Edition. Norwich: TSO (The Stationery Office) for AXELOS Ltd, 2009.

Martin, D.D. and Shell, R.L. *Management of Professionals.* New York: Marcel Dekker, Inc, 1988.

Mazza, C., Fairclough, J., Melton, B., De Pablo, D., Scheffer, A. and Stevens, R. *Software Engineering Standards.* Hemel Hempstead: Prentice Hall, 1994.

Mazza, C., Fairclough, J., Melton, B., De Pablo, D., Scheffer, A., Stevens, R., Jones, M. and Alvisi, G. *Software Engineering Guides.* Hemel Hempstead: Prentice Hall, 1996.

Mehrabian, A. *Nonverbal Communication.* Piscataway, NJ: Aldine Transaction, a division of Transaction Publishers, 2007.

Portfolio, Programme and Project Offices. Norwich: TSO (The Stationery Office) for AXELOS Ltd, 2013.

Purba, S. and Zucchero, J.J. *Project Rescue.* Emeryville, CA: McGraw-Hill/ Osborne, 2004.

Remenyi, D., Money, A., Sherwood-smith, M. and Irani, Z. *The Effective Measurement and Management of IT Costs and Benefits.* Oxford: Butterworth-Heinemann, 2000.

Rummler, G.A. and Brache, A.P. *Improving Performance.* San Francisco, CA: Jossey-Bass Inc, 1995.

Schwaber, K. and Sutherland, J. 2013. 'The Scrum Guide'. Available at: http://www.scrumguides.org.

Slack, N., Brandon-Jones, A., Johnston, R. and Betts, A. *Operations and Process Management*, 3rd edn. Harlow: Pearson Education, 2012.

Spenley, P. *World Class Performance through Total Quality.* London: Chapman & Hall, 1992.

Tuckman, B.W. 'Developmental Sequence in Small Groups'. *Psychological Bulletin*, 63(6) (1965), 384–99, published by the American Psychological Association (APA), referenced with permission.

Walsh, C. *Key Management Ratios.* Harlow: Pearson Education, 2006.

Wilson, B. *Soft Systems Methodology.* Chichester: John Wiley & Sons, 2004.

Wilson, J.M. 'Gantt Charts: A Centenary Appreciation'. *European Journal of Operational Research*, 149 (2003), 430–37.

Index